Advance Praise

"Medical breakthroughs garner applause for doctors. But these scientific battles take place in the bodies of patients—they're the ones who put their lives, emotions, and financial resources on the line. In *Unstoppable*, Ellen Casey's beautiful prose sweeps us along on her journey as a pioneering patient undergoing in vitro fertilization. Her grit, persuasiveness, investigative skills, bravery, and inability to take no for an answer made her dream of parenthood come true. Her story will inspire you, no matter what your particular dream may be."

—**Lori Andrews**, lawyer, bioethicist, and author of *The Clone Age: Adventures in the World of Reproductive Technology*

"Ellen Casey's story of resilience is a remarkable one."

—**Ann V. Klotz**, head at Laurel School for Girls; founder of Laurel's Center for Research on Girls, blogger for *Huffington Post*, writer, and teacher

"This story is about pioneering gynecology in part, but, more significantly, it is the story of one woman's courage and perseverance in her quest to become a mother. Anyone experiencing infertility should find inspiration and hope here."

—**John M. Smith**, MD, author of *Women and Doctors*

"As a modern-day mother of an IVF 'test tube' baby, I felt the stress and anguish of desperately wanting a baby and being unable to conceive on my own. Fortunately, today's doctors have the experience and knowledge of millions of babies born using in vitro fertilization. Ellen Casey had to experience that grief and longing, while also pioneering a brand new assisted reproductive technology and facing the immense scrutiny and judgment of being in the public eye. This book shares the story of a woman's longing to be a mother and the exhaustive journey it would take to get there."

—**Kimberly Miller**, IVF mother

"Ellen's remarkable story is one of grit, courage, and, finally, triumph. An IVF mother myself, I was captivated by the magnitude of her journey as a true pioneer in fertility medicine. This inspiring book is not to miss for anyone who can appreciate the marvels of science and the power of a mother's love."

—**Beth P. Finch**, IVF mother

Unstoppable

With warm wishes,
John W. Casey

A MEMOIR

Unstoppable

FORGING THE PATH
TO MOTHERHOOD IN THE
EARLY DAYS OF IVF

ELLEN WEIR CASEY

RIVER GROVE
BOOKS

Published by River Grove Books
Austin, TX
www.rivergrovebooks.com

Distributed by River Grove Books

Design and composition by Greenleaf Book Group
Cover design by Greenleaf Book Group
Cover images used under license from
©Shutterstock.com/Yurko Gud, ©Shutterstock.com/Flas100
Author photo by Kira Whitney

Publisher's Cataloging-in-Publication data is available.

Print ISBN: 978-1-63299-497-4

eBook ISBN: 978-1-63299-498-1

First Edition

For Elizabeth and Peter

I live in eternal gratitude to these medical geniuses whose innovative brilliance helped me have our precious baby daughter, "Colorado's first test-tube baby."

Dr. Martin M. Quigley

Dr. Victor Gomel

Dr. Michael Baggish

Dr. John Smith

Dr. Patrick Steptoe

Dr. Robert G. Edwards

"I know they really wanted me."

—Elizabeth, age ten, *Colorado Springs Gazette*

*"I told my class today that I was a test-tube baby.
I explained exactly how it worked. They didn't believe me.
I guess they'll just figure it out someday."*

—Elizabeth, age eight

*"Mommy, I can't remember. Is he the doctor
who put me in or took me out?"*

—On the way to visit the doctor who delivered her,
Elizabeth, age five

Author's Note

I believe women today should know the stories of the women who went before them, not so very long ago. These were pioneering women who startled convention by questioning authority, who did their own research, made their own decisions, talked about difficult, taboo subjects, and paved the way for you, the brave, independent-thinking, goal-driven females whom we so respect and value today.

I was one of those pioneers. I was unable to have a child because a medical doctor endangered my health by presenting me with an experimental IUD, not approved by the FDA. This book is the story of what I endured in the earliest days of infertility treatment, both medically and emotionally, as well as the cultural, informational, and religious roadblocks I faced.

Writing this book was both exhilarating and heartbreaking as I relived devastating losses and extreme successes. This is my very personal story and the memories are mine alone. I used my copious files, which I began compiling in 1979, and was able to refer to medical bills, dates of appointments, notes on procedures, paper airplane tickets, letters, and documents from medical offices. This was such a help in confirming my recollection of facts, addresses, and dates.

Each conversation and situation is as I remember it; others may recall details differently. Memory is a tricky thing, and I represent this as solely my own experience. I have changed names and identifying characteristics of every person except for my own, my husband's, Sylvia Pace-Owens, and the spectacular doctors, each of whom did his best to help us to have a child. There was so much I did not know at the time about the nascent IVF, other types of surgery, and the possibility of complications. I have researched and spoken to today's medical specialists to fill in details.

I am elated to know that young women today have options for treatment performed by experienced specialists to help them achieve their dream of becoming mothers. I also know how agonizingly hard this road is and hope my story will give each one hope that she, too, will have a happy ending.

—Ellen W. Casey

April 1984

"Wouldn't you say you are playing God?" the talk show host hissed, leaning her heavily made-up face right into mine as if to challenge me.

The Boston-based television show had just gone live. I was one of four guests, seated in a chair to the host's right. In my peripheral vision I noticed the experts on the panel with me freeze in response to the host's aggressive posturing. Two medical doctors, a bioethics lawyer, and I had been briefed, moments before the cameras rolled, on the host's plan for her hour-long show. First, the professionals were to explain the medical and legal details of in vitro fertilization. Then, the host said, I was to be the final person interviewed and would describe my baby.

This was definitely not the plan she had shared with us. Her first question was an arrow aimed at me.

"Wouldn't you say you are playing God?"

In an instant I recognized that she was attempting to ambush me with the massive religious and ethical controversy surrounding what were then called "test-tube babies." If she had known what I'd been through over the past five years, she would have realized I wouldn't shatter at her attempt to rattle me.

I had been clear about why I accepted the invitation to travel to Boston from Colorado Springs and appear on this television program. It was important to me to let other couples know that they now had the chance to have their own baby. The minute I knew I was safely three months pregnant with one of the world's first test-tube babies, I had called my doctor in Houston to tell him that I would speak to anyone: the press, prospective or current patients, anyone he chose. I made a bargain with God to share this new and successful method of conception.

In vitro fertilization was still so rare in the early 1980s, and most people regarded so-called test-tube babies as something out of science fiction. The general public did not understand the mechanisms of the experimental procedure at all, and I felt an overwhelming obligation to help educate them. I also wanted to protect my baby, Elizabeth, from being regarded as an anomaly, a curiosity, not a perfectly normal, desperately wanted child. If my efforts were successful today, Elizabeth would never have to defend her conception as a terrifying beginning of a brave new world.

I hoped that when women heard my story, they would be inspired to never give up on their own dreams to become mothers.

I wasn't playing God. I was on television because I had a story to tell.

Chapter 1

"Well, Ellen, you can't get pregnant."

Dr. Maxim walked into the room where I waited, talking as he crossed the floor. His starched white coat was so stiff it didn't move as it brushed my knees. I sat in a narrow exam room on a small chair, next to a desk. My doctor wasn't looking at me. He tossed my file folder onto his desk. It sounded like a slap. He plopped heavily into his seat. In a flat voice, devoid of emotion, he added, "The test shows that your Fallopian tubes are 100 percent blocked."

I felt my brain stop, like it had when I was fifteen and my father told me in a stricken voice that Granny Bessie had died. Then, that was the most unbearable jolt I had endured in my lifetime. This blow now felt exactly the same.

Shock seared my brain, and then everything became impossibly still around me. It sounded like I was underwater or had my hands cupped over my ears. There was no air to breathe, nothing moved. I could not survive this. I was done. Living without a child was incomprehensible—a cruelly absurd fate for a kindergarten teacher like me whose life was centered on children.

Just minutes earlier, I'd held my breath while Dr. Maxim squeezed blue dye through a syringe into my uterus as I lay on a metal cart. The dye was supposed to flow easily through my Fallopian tubes, but it did not even manage to seep into them at all. My fingernails dug into the palms of both clenched fists. The pressure caused a mean pain that ripped through me. I pictured gnarled claws squeezing and squeezing my ovaries. I stared up at the holes in the acoustic ceiling tiles above me in an attempt to take my mind off the agony.

"Stop," I gasped. The doctor looked through his glasses at me, over my raised knees that were covered by a draped white sheet. He turned his head to gaze at an X-ray type image on a small screen. I looked, too, and saw the dye had pooled in the shape of a heart.

"This hurts because the dye has stopped at the opening to the Fallopian tubes," he said with a slightly negative motion of his head. "What you see on the screen is the shape of your uterus. If I continue putting pressure on the tubes, they just might pop open."

I frowned at his supercilious use of the word "pop." It was cavalier. I wondered if he had any idea how tortuous this pain felt to me. Did doctors learn what anguish this procedure inflicted on a woman while they were in medical school? He certainly did not give off one note of empathy in his matter-of-fact tone.

"Okay, keep trying," I said quickly, then rushed to suck enough air into my lungs and hold it there tightly, before the torment could restart.

• • •

My guilt helped me press the air down harder onto my diaphragm. I stared up at the dots on the ceiling tile again and tried to focus on counting them instead of feeling the pain. I knew this was my fault.

A few years out of college, in 1974, I thought that getting an experimental IUD was a great idea. It had seemed almost daring to me at the time. I always took risks, but calculated risks. The doctor never mentioned the possibility that the material being tested in the IUD could be dangerous to the body of a twenty-four-year-old woman, and I had no idea it posed a risk. The only form of female birth control I knew about then was "the pill."

I remember the Friday afternoon my Uncle Jack sauntered into his house wearing green golf slacks and laughing. It was 1962, and I was a sheltered thirteen-year-old girl attending private school. I was lounging on a couch in my green school uniform listening to my mother and two aunts talk about Jackie Kennedy's White House tour that we all had watched on television. Uncle Jack had laughter in his voice when he told my aunt that the plastic container he was holding, given to him by an obstetrician golfing buddy, was the best thing ever invented. I noticed amusement flash across the faces of my two aunts and my mother, but I had no idea what was in that blue thing that was the size of my retainer case. He presented Aunt

Helen with the little round box. On our drive home, my mom told me that it held the new birth control pill. I felt my face immediately flush. We lived just a few blocks from my cousins' home, and I was so grateful that she didn't have time to launch into a discussion of sex and birth control before we pulled into the garage and I jumped out of the car.

One evening during my freshman year in college, the girls in my dorm lay across beds, wearing pink foam rollers and pajamas, talking. A girl named Ann complained, in a sort of bragging way, that "the pill" caused her to gain weight and gave her headaches. I was fascinated. I wasn't about to have sex at that point; college was the first time I had ever gone to school with boys. I was having fun dating fraternity guys, going to their beer busts in the mountains and skiing with them. Sex would irreversibly create an emotional attachment, my mom warned me, but it wouldn't be the same for the boy.

That kind of attachment was the last thing I wanted. I had a list of everything I wanted to do, like hear the crunch of snow under my boots as I stepped onto the continent of Antarctica, write a children's book for girls, stroll slowly in the Giacometti sculpture garden in the south of France, and smell the damp rock walls inside the Pantheon. Some of these girls in my dorm seemed so much older than I was, so I just sat silent and listened carefully.

Years later, I was twenty-four years old when I talked to a gynecologist in his office in Colorado Springs. I was so embarrassed to have to discuss birth control with a man that I almost canceled the appointment. My face felt moist. I tried to mask my self-consciousness by presenting myself as an intellectual adult. I even tried to lower my voice to sound more grown up.

4

"You are correct, the pill does have side effects," silver-haired Dr. Maxim said formally while folding his hands together in agreement. "The most common ones are headache and weight gain. Some more serious complications, such as blood clots and, of course, pregnancy, do rarely occur." He was responding to the questions I read off of a list written in my green spiral notebook.

"What other options are there other than the pill?" I asked in the lowest, most serious voice I could manage. I couldn't believe I was having this conversation. "I understand that there are some new medical advances."

"Actually, I have an exciting brochure right here," he said, as he handed me a lightweight pamphlet from a stack on a round table near his chair. I looked at the paper flopping limply in my hand, expecting to see a serious medical description. Instead, the front cover had a color picture of a teenage girl and boy sitting on a lawn, his hand on hers, smiling at each other. I didn't know whether to laugh at the clichéd photo or to bolt out the door. I certainly did not want to sit there one second more. "This information describes a new IUD. It is an intrauterine device in the latest material and shape. It is inserted, mostly painlessly, through the woman's cervix into her uterus. Once it is there, pregnancy cannot occur. There are no side effects except mild cramping after insertion."

"How, exactly, does it prevent conception?" I asked, hoping I sounded like the graduate student I was. I was forcing my foot to stop nervously tapping the floor.

"The IUD is a foreign object and creates friction so that an egg cannot implant in the uterine wall." If he had correctly said "a fertilized egg," I know I would have been shocked and probably never have proceeded. He did not answer my question, so I continued to think an IUD blocked pregnancy from occurring.

He kept talking rapidly, like a salesman. "You are an excellent candidate for this, since you do not want the side effects of the pill." He stood up, turning his back to me. "I should also mention that I have been chosen to conduct this experiment for the Global Health Council." His voice was hard to hear as he walked across the room to his desk. He picked up a form and a pen and walked back across the carpet toward me. "I am one of the few physicians selected to test this new IUD for contraception. And the only doctor in Colorado Springs, of course, to be a part of this."

I registered his haughty undertone. Still, I was a smart, educated twenty-four-year-old and was intellectually seduced to learn that my doctor was chosen to conduct an important scientific study. He had to be an excellent physician.

The experimental IUD sounded perfect. "No side effects," he had said. I bent over the short release form, ready to take my part in this controlled trial to help young women just like me. You would think the act of signing on the line, never imagining I was actually signing away my life's dream of having a baby, would have felt momentous. In a movie there would have been ominous music playing in low tones in the background. But there in that office, I simply wrote my name and clicked the button on the end of the ballpoint pen.

How was it that I never sensed the danger?

Two short months later I arrived at the emergency room with a 103-degree fever fueled by an infection raging inside of my uterus, caused by the IUD.

. . .

"Don't worry." Dr. Maxim's inane phrase rocketed me out of my IUD memory and back into the surreal present. I knew how conception worked. The human egg was fertilized in the Fallopian tubes, then traveled downward through them to the uterus, where the embryo implanted in the uterine wall to begin a pregnancy. Blocked Fallopian tubes meant conception could not occur.

I could not have a baby.

My ears buzzed. My hands shook. The room still echoed with his earlier words, "You can't get pregnant." I took a huge breath to stay alive in this moment.

Then he said, "I can do surgery to open the Fallopian tubes, no problem."

I couldn't respond. How did he assume he could perform such a specialized surgery? Had he done it before? I looked up from my chair, my panicked eyes searching the doctor's face for some hope.

But he was still not looking at me.

Everything inside the room froze, including me. The doctor dissolved from my vision and my brain moved swiftly into survival mode. I knew from the bit of research I had done prior to today's procedure that no general obstetric surgeon could successfully perform the delicate tubal surgery I now knew I required to get pregnant. I had been secretly concerned for years that the IUD infection had caused damage, which was why I scheduled this dye test. I hadn't gotten pregnant after four months of marriage, and my instinct told me something was very wrong. Peter and I were both twenty-nine years old, and we only had until age thirty-five before entering the danger zone for conception. After thirty-five, "genetic abnormalities" became a risk for the baby. Down syndrome was the main fetal defect that could be diagnosed by amniocentesis.

"No problem," he said again, suggesting an easy success that I suspected did not exist. He thought he could perform surgery to open the tiny Fallopian tubes. I was speechless at this local doctor's tone and was thankful for my education, which had taught me to question power and confidently search for my own answers. I thought of all the women who had been raised to take a doctor's word without question—including me just a few years ago.

A family was all I ever wanted. A mother was what I was meant to be.

Politely, I requested the name of an infertility specialist for a second opinion, someone at the University of Colorado Hospital in Denver. I left the building in a daze of rapid thoughts, ironically holding a piece of paper with a birth control pill company's name printed at the top, torn from a pad on the doctor's desk. I never saw that doctor again.

• • •

I had to take absolute control over my own physical care. I vowed to research every bit of medical information and find out which innovative doctors were performing new treatments that could help me. I was confident that I would do anything to have a baby. I had no idea how many long days I would soon spend doing library research. I didn't know that I would have surgery eight times in the next four years in three different states and in one Canadian province. The knee-buckling agony of loss, the physical pain, paralyzing grief, and the front-page headlines were all looming in the months ahead.

Magnificent Pikes Peak—pink granite covered with snow—towered over me in the west as I stood outside the brick medical building. I recalled being so exhausted after climbing that iconic mountain last September with my husband, Peter, that I could barely walk the next day.

I hadn't told Peter about this test today, and I wasn't going to tell him anything about this problem until I had found the solution. I had to make this right.

I stood up as straight as I could and trudged toward my yellow VW bug. I had only felt this starkly alone once before in my life. That was the day I picked up my darling stepfather's autopsy report from the New Canaan coroner's office. "Alone, alone, alone," my shoes had squeaked aloud as I made my way down the station stairs that day. I heard the same words now with each step as I moved blindly across the pavement.

Early Birth Control from 1960 to 1974

When I was in my early twenties, the only information I could get on birth control was from friends or my doctor. The information from my contemporaries was unreliable and my doctors were caught between the release of new methods of contraception, the controversy over their use, and the disastrous results from some—including infection and death. Birth control was illegal for unmarried women in the United States until 1972, a year after I graduated from college.

1916—Margaret Sanger coined the term "birth control" and opened the first birth control clinic in Brooklyn, NY. In 1917, a court judged her "guilty of maintaining a public nuisance" and she was sentenced to thirty days in jail.

1960—The birth control pill was approved by the FDA.

1965—The Supreme Court ruled that married couples had the right to use birth control, nullifying the Comstock Act of 1873, which prohibited distribution of, and advertising about, birth control.

1968—The FDA approved intrauterine devices (IUDs).

1972—The Supreme Court ruled that birth control was legal for all US citizens, married or not.

1974—The FDA suspended sale of the Dalkon Shield, an IUD that caused severe infections and death.

Chapter 2

I stepped into the University of Colorado Hospital and stood still for a moment, as if I were invisible. It seemed I had entered a scene from a film. Solemn patients in patterned gowns were being pushed in wheelchairs, knees covered with white cotton blankets. Most kept their eyes down, looking at the floor ahead or at their own laps. Visitors carried vases of flowers bought from the hospital gift shop and talked to each other in low tones. Were they speaking so quietly out of respect for the hospital or out of fear? People squinted trying to read lists of departments and floors from signs next to the elevators. Two workers beyond orange caution cones bent over, dipped their gray mops into metal buckets, then hurled long splatters across the linoleum floor. I flinched at the strong smell of ammonia as I passed.

I had entered a foreign, uncomfortable world. The atmosphere felt very different from places where strangers normally pass each other, like shopping malls, airports, or grocery stores. Not one person laughed aloud. Even children holding an adult's hand were subdued. Everyone looked lost, uncertain of which way to go. I assured myself that I knew where I was going. "I am not sick," I told myself. I looked again at the paper in my hand after pushing the up button for the elevator. I focused on the round yellow lights showing the descending elevators. I knew exactly where I was going—to see the doctor whose name I had been given for a second opinion.

There was a substitute teacher in my kindergarten classroom that day, and I hoped my Thursday parent volunteers had shown up to help her. I sat down in the waiting room and reached for the professional periodicals. I searched each magazine's table of contents for the words "tubal blockage, tubal surgery." I did not see a single article on the topic, but there were some on infertility. I had to find the top specialists in the world doing the newest, most successful procedures on blocked Fallopian tubes. I felt it was up to me to find the smartest infertility doctors in Colorado and talk to them for advice and referrals. That is why I was here. As I looked through these journals, I jotted down the names of authors of pertinent articles I found, and hospitals where the newest research was being done.

My name was called by the physician's assistant, and I was led into the specialist's office. The doctor was waiting for me behind his office desk, which let me know he had paid attention to the specific appointment I'd scheduled. I did not need another examination. I needed help and educated advice. I handed him my file with the results of my dye test. Under my arm I clasped a giant, thin envelope holding the X-ray films. I knew that the name of that horrid dye test was a hysterosalpingogram. That term was the beginning of my new medical vocabulary, which increased impressively over the next four years of trying to conceive. That very specific vocabulary of reproductive procedures and terms remains in my lexicon today, thirty-seven years later.

This doctor was an infertility professional. It was a small, specialized field and I was so glad to have his name and get this appointment. He placed reading glasses low on his nose to carefully peruse the report. Then he stood and flipped on a light that illuminated a wall pocket where he dropped in my X-ray films, one at a time. He, of course, knew it was impossible to become pregnant when both Fallopian tubes were blocked, something the films clearly showed.

He turned off the light, sat back in his chair, and we discussed my options for surgery to open the tubes. He raised his eyebrows when I mentioned the Colorado Springs doctor had said he could do the surgery, confirming my own reaction at the time. Only two doctors in the world were having success with surgery on Fallopian tubes, he told me seriously. They were each trying microsurgery. He wrote down three names and contact numbers for me. The top name on the list was Dr. John Smith, an ob-gyn specialist in Colorado Springs. The other two names were the doctors he had just mentioned who were successfully operating on Fallopian tubes: Dr. Victor Gomel of Vancouver, Canada, and the renowned Dr. Steptoe of England. Dr. Patrick Steptoe, along with physiologist

Dr. Robert Edwards, had pioneered the conception and 1978 birth of the world's first "Test-Tube Baby," Louise Brown. I immediately recognized Dr. Steptoe's name.

• • •

"But, Peter, look what the doctor in Denver gave me today," I would say when I got home. "I have the names and phone numbers of the only two doctors in the world who are doing successful microsurgery to open blocked Fallopian tubes. Can you believe this? I have their phone numbers." Then I would snap the paper loudly in the air. For the entire hour-and-a-half drive back home from Denver, I rehearsed this conversation. It was crucial to have Peter understand. It was critical that he allow me to have the surgery. I had to present this to him precisely and professionally—and convincingly.

Peter was sitting on our couch in Chipita Park, the mountain town outside of Colorado Springs where we lived. Our contemporary house was built down the side of the mountain so that each of the three levels was suspended over the tops of the giant blue spruce trees soaring up from the rocky soil below. I always thought our house on stilts looked like the old mines we saw higher in the mountains. This was the life I had always pictured: Peter and me inside a Colorado home with enormous windows, contemporary art on the walls, and a baby playing with wooden Swedish toys on a quilt on the floor. Even on our honeymoon in Tahiti, as we lounged by the aqua hotel pool, we imagined having babies—even mused about what we would name our children. Peter liked Tim for a boy. I was surprised and charmed that he had already been thinking of becoming a father.

Peter had arrived home from work a half hour earlier. I gave him as much time to settle in as I could stand before I sat softly on the couch next to him and explained that I had a problem with my Fallopian tubes and had gone to a specialist in Denver that day.

I jumped up and stood in front of the windows before giving him the good news contained on the paper I held. My plan had been to wait to tell him there was a problem until I had a "plan B" for us. Tonight I had exactly that.

"Okay," he answered, finishing a tortilla chip that he had just dipped into hot sauce. He seemed puzzled by the contrast between this disturbing information and my excited voice, but he was at a disadvantage. I had known about my tubal blockage for two weeks, and I had not included him in the panic I had been living in since first visiting Dr. Maxim. Peter was just hearing about it for the first time.

I stood in the middle of the living room, talking too quickly. I was afraid to pause and risk opening the air so that he could ask questions. I was firing off questions like "Which doctor should we choose for microsurgery?" and "Which clinic should I call first?" Peter looked serious and didn't move at all. It was clear that I was absolutely determined to find a way for us to have our own baby. I talked about the logistics, from even being able to reach these international clinics by long-distance phone, to being screened and accepted into a microsurgery program. What was microsurgery and was it safe? Would our insurance cover surgery outside of the US?

Peter slowly dipped a chip into the salsa bowl. I saw drops of red fall onto the napkin on his knee as he lifted the chip to his mouth. He still hadn't spoken another word. He clearly needed time to digest this onslaught of information. I stopped talking.

"Ellen, what is this going to cost us? I can see that you are serious here. You are talking about traveling to two foreign countries for surgery." He shook his head in a "no" motion.

"Peter, I am going. This is our only chance to have a baby. These are the best doctors in the world." Fear cracked my voice as I added, "Do you think either of them will let me into the microsurgery trials?"

Peter shook his head side to side, musing. "Ellen, if anyone can get herself in, it is you."

That was all I needed to hear, as much of a green light as Peter was going to voice. He was naturally quiet and reserved. I learned early on in our relationship that his silence wasn't a bad sign. He was kind, cerebral, and calm; a man of few words. When we were dating, I made lists of questions to ask him that did not have yes or no answers to try to draw the reserved object of my affection into conversation. It gave him a bit of a mysterious air, which I loved. His few, carefully chosen words were always brilliant and funny.

The very next morning I sat on my bedside before dressing for work and dialed the number of Dr. Victor Gomel in Canada. I called so early that the taped message advised me his office wouldn't open for another three hours.

Chapter 3

"You are turning heads," Peter said with an amused smile. I was swinging my arms as I walked like a child proudly marching up to claim an award from the principal. I had on chocolate-brown suede culottes, a striped nubby-knit sweater, brown tights, and tall boots. My mother had mailed this outfit to me from her home in Connecticut over a month ago. I had saved it to wear for something special. Today was that something special.

We had just stepped off the plane and were inside the airport in Vancouver, Canada. I walked with the stride and attitude of a young woman who felt her deepest dreams right under her feet. We were finally here, on our way to see Dr. Victor Gomel. I heard self-assurance in each strong click of my boot heels on the stone floors. Boots made me feel powerful. I held my head like I was famous.

My attitude was what was attracting passing glances from strangers, not my outfit. I just couldn't stop smiling.

The red Canadian maple leaf was on display everywhere as our taxi drove through the streets of the city that autumn day. Neither of us had ever been to Vancouver. We loved visiting new places, and that added to the excitement of being accepted to meet with this hyper-specialized doctor. We had waited five months for this appointment with Dr. Gomel. I felt euphoric to be here and shivered with an excited rush. We asked the driver to tour us around the city a bit before dropping us at the hotel. The driver pointed out Gastown as we passed between red-brick buildings with green-and-white painted trim. Menu boards sat outside restaurants with colored awnings. Storefront shop windows held green soapstone, Eskimo carvings, Hudson's Bay blankets, old mustard-glass bowls, woolen mittens and sweaters. Some of the buildings had ornate, newly painted porticos. It looked like a rough Victorian neighborhood that had been made into a tourist district. We saw the famous Steam Clock with faces on the three sides we could see from the passing taxi window. It looked like an enormous grandfather clock made of metal, which apparently blew steam out of its top on the hour. It felt like we were driving through a movie set, but all I could really focus on was tomorrow's appointment.

• • •

"I know this is my fault," I screamed silently to myself the next day as I reached for the arm of the chair to sit down. I quickly gulped for air in a panic, hoping that no one noticed. I could feel my hands shaking. "I am the one who used the IUD. I am the one who ruined this for us. My fault. My fault. My fault." I shook my head to whisk away the thoughts that were overtaking me like amorphous spirits in a horror film. My confidence had dissolved.

Peter and I sat next to each other across from Dr. Victor Gomel. He smiled without showing his teeth, which had the resulting effect of the warmth of his eyes being even more intense. His was one of the names I'd been given by the infertility specialist at the University of Colorado Hospital in Denver. Dr. Gomel was one of the two doctors in the world doing successful microsurgery on Fallopian tubes, and I had persevered through phone calls and letters, and had X-ray films mailed to him by my doctors, to get this appointment.

It was Monday of Thanksgiving week in late November, and this was the beginning of my vacation. I was a kindergarten teacher at Rudy Elementary School in Colorado Springs. The population and building surge on the eastern side of the city had overcrowded the elementary schools. It was darkly ironic that the schools had too many children, yet I could not have a baby. To accommodate the rush of students, the newest schools, like mine, opened using an innovative block schedule. There were three patterns, each running for twelve and a half weeks followed by a four-week break. Research showed that shorter breaks resulted in greater retention of reading and math skills. The Friday before my vacation, I took down all of the brown construction-paper turkeys flying from the classroom ceiling and sent them home with the children's turkey finger paintings and construction-paper Pilgrim hats and collars. I had taken an entire roll of film of my little five-year-olds, dressed as Pilgrims and Indians for the Thanksgiving feast that the room mothers served. I couldn't wait until we returned from Canada to pick up the developed photos—pictures of little round faces in Pilgrim hats. Their chubby, smooth cheeks tore at my heart. All I wanted was to be able to wipe baby food off of my own baby's round, pink cheeks.

My teaching block had ended on Friday, and we hopped on a plane Sunday morning. I was giddily certain that this tubal surgery would result in us being able to have our own baby. Peter seemed to be gladly riding on the wake of my confidence, like a water-skier holding on behind a speedboat. As I sat in my chair, I tried to take everything in: the doctor's curly, dark hair, his intense eyes, the folders and papers on his desk. I had hand-delivered a formal letter requesting Dr. Maxim's office mail my medical records to Dr. Gomel. The results of that excruciating dye test I had undergone in April were now in front of us on his desk. I recognized the letterhead. The X-ray films, mailed separately in an oversized manila envelope, clearly showed the blockage at the opening of each Fallopian tube where it should have opened into the uterus. If all went well today as expected, my surgery would be on Wednesday. If the surgery was successful, I would have two completely cleared Fallopian tubes.

The damage I had caused would be gone.

Some minutes later I was in Dr. Gomel's private examination room with two nurses. I had been allowed the dignity of keeping my sweater on and only needed the sheet to cover my lower body. This room felt different from the impersonal exam rooms I had seen in Colorado. A nurse used long tongs to pull what looked like washcloths from a metal box on the countertop. They were warmed covers for the stirrups at the end of the examination table. I couldn't believe it. The insult of having to place our bare feet into cold metal stirrups for every gynecological exam was shared by all women. When she placed them over the metal, and I slipped my feet into heated padding, I couldn't believe it. I immediately relaxed a bit.

"Dr. Gomel is amazing. He does so much to make his patients feel more comfortable," she said. The other nurse nodded in agreement.

"I had an experimental IUD for just two months. I got a terrible infection from it. I had a high fever and cramps and could barely walk into the doctor's office to have it removed," I told Dr. Gomel following a brief internal exam. "This is my fault." The words caught in my throat and I dared myself to not cry.

Peter didn't know about the IUD. He hadn't asked and I hadn't brought it up. His reticence, for once, was a positive for me. He hadn't verbally queried me about what had caused my scarring, and I was grateful. My guilt was like a knife inside me, and while I would never lie to Peter, it seemed that "I had a bad infection" was all he cared to know. I was terrified that he might blame me for what I had done.

I have to make it better. Oh, God, I am so sorry. All I have ever wanted is a baby. Did I say the words aloud, or just think them? I didn't dare appear desperate to this doctor. What if he wouldn't do the surgery on me?

"The fault is not yours," Dr. Gomel replied, leaning forward. He looked right at me through dark-brown eyes, above which sat thick, heavy eyebrows.

"The IUD was the only medical option other than the pill at the time. However, suggesting this method of contraception to an unmarried girl who has no children yet is inexcusable." I saw that he was angry about the devastating internal damage that had been caused, resulting in my current inability to conceive. He was holding my hand. He breathed in deeply, going on to explain again the microsurgical procedure he would perform. His diction was cultured and beautiful, his voice calm. This was not my fault? I needed to think about that later. My hope regained its place on firm ground as it pushed away my omnipresent guilt.

Peter and I walked out the office door into the gray Vancouver rain twenty minutes later. "I know this is going to work," I said firmly. "I really like him and have complete confidence in his ability to do my surgery tomorrow." Peter did not respond at all. I couldn't gauge if he was concerned that I was too hopeful and could be crushed if the surgery didn't work or if he was just silently considering the medical information we had been given. He just opened his umbrella and we got into the waiting taxi.

• • •

It was late afternoon of the following day, but I didn't know that. I didn't know where I was. I didn't remember that I had just had surgery.

I tried to see but immediately slammed my eyes shut in shock. The light was sharply blinding, making me think of the sun glaring off the snow on the ski slopes when I removed my sunglasses. But I didn't smell the usual fresh, crisp air of the mountains. And nothing sounded right either. I tried to gather myself to figure out where I was.

I slowly opened my eyelids partway and peeked through a gauzy curtain. I closed my eyes again, as nothing made sense. It was just too much effort to try to resist the pull of sleep.

Sometime later I heard a female voice say my name loudly. "Ellen, time to wake up. Ellen, I have brought you some water. Are you thirsty? Open your eyes and have a sip. Ellen?"

Like an obedient child, I responded to my name and complied by opening my eyes. A nurse slipped a straw with accordion pleats into my mouth. On a vague level I registered that we called them magic straws when I was a child. She must have walked away after my second sip and I again closed my eyes. But now, I was trying harder to hold on to being awake. I was alone in a room with curtains for side walls. I could see that there was a much larger room in front of mine. I saw curtained spaces like slots holding other, unmoving patients beyond that. The room had metal cabinets, and rolling carts went by being pushed by people in white. They were so distant, and I was so far away. So far away.

"I have brought you a warm blanket," said a gentle voice, awakening me again. I was swathed in warmth as fingers tucked heated fabric under my shoulders, torso, and legs. I felt comfortable and taken care of, slipping back into a light sleep that was soon disturbed. "We are going to take you into the Recovery Room now," someone announced loudly, like I was deaf. The sides of my bed were loudly pulled up and jerked into place. One person stood behind me and another was at my feet. As they wheeled my bed, the wheels rattled in protest beneath me. I couldn't look up, as the movement made me feel slightly sick and dizzy.

"Here she is!" a voice I thought I recognized as the water-giver's said brightly.

"Hi, there, sweet E," Peter said, settling into a chair next to me. "How do you feel?"

"I don't know," I heard myself answer, in a voice like an echo. "Weird." I had never had surgery before and continued to try to force my brain to become clearer. But enough fog had cleared away that I was aware of the day's goal. I asked, "Did it work?"

Just then, Dr. Gomel pulled back the curtain at the foot of my bed. "You did just beautifully," his kind voice said. "Your surgery lasted far longer than expected due to the extensive internal scarring. I was only able to work on one tube during that time, due to the extent of the scar tissue. The good news is that your left Fallopian tube is clear now. Get some rest and I will visit you in the morning, first thing."

Peter walked out with Dr. Gomel and I heard them talking. To my relief, he soon returned to sit in his chair next to me. I wanted Peter right there with me as I fought for release from this strange, suspended consciousness. I was aware that I couldn't think and remember right now, so I trusted Peter to think for both of us. I felt a wisp of relief that I didn't have to be in charge.

Chapter 4

"Good morning." It was the day after the microsurgery. I opened my eyes and there stood Dr. Gomel, smiling at the foot of my bed, a nurse next to him holding a clipboard. Peter got up from his chair, laying down his paperback biography of Disraeli. They shook hands almost formally, then both turned to me.

"How is everything down below?" asked Dr. Gomel brightly as he walked up next to me. His turn of phrase made me want to giggle.

But I had no time to waste, so quickly became serious and anxious. The morning sun shone in bright swaths across the floor. I desperately needed to know exactly what had happened in the operating room yesterday. I vaguely remembered Dr. Gomel patting my hand in the recovery room and speaking to me, but his words were not clear in my anesthesia-dazed memory. It was like trying to remember a dream too many hours after waking.

I held my breath, eager to hear every specific detail he could give me. All I wanted to know was if we could have a baby. Had the surgeon been able to open my Fallopian tubes? It was like waiting to hear if I would live or die.

Dr. Gomel calmly reminded me that the surgery had included significant time spent excising massive uterine adhesions. He had succeeded in opening the left Fallopian tube. Now I remembered hearing this from him yesterday. Only one tube was open, but that was enough; I could get pregnant. This was all I needed to know. My life could go on, and Peter and I would have our children.

A second nurse, whom I hadn't even noticed in the background, pulled the yellow privacy curtains separating my bed from the patient still sleeping next to me. I had seen an unconscious woman, with an IV cart attached to her, wheeled into my room earlier that morning. Dr. Gomel's nurse, whom I recognized from my office exam two days earlier, carefully removed the dressing from my lower stomach. I noticed that she and the doctor stood on the far side of my bed so that only they, and not Peter, could see my exposed wound. I appreciated the discretion. I never wanted Peter to know how badly this inability to conceive had impacted me emotionally. I just couldn't bear for him to know how brokenhearted I really was. Now he was thankfully shielded from seeing the immediate physical results of yesterday's seven-hour surgery as well. I wanted to protect him.

Yesterday's microsurgery had been performed using the new technology of the laparoscope—a slim, lighted tube with a camera at the end that sent pictures to a screen that my surgeon could view. The incision through which the tiny tools and laparoscope were inserted was made through my navel. I did not know at the time that Dr. Gomel was the first physician in Canada to use the laparoscope in his experimental microsurgery on Fallopian tubes.

This morning my abdomen was still bloated and enormous from the gas that had been pumped inside to make room for the doctor's movements during surgery. In a private wish, I imagined my belly was really domed because I was pregnant. My skin was stained a rust color around the bandages. I did not need to see my incision, as the sight of the horrifyingly enormous stomach had already upset me a bit. I focused instead on cracks above in the plastered ceiling. The doctor checked out the incision both carefully and quickly. The nurse gently laid the bandages back, pressing the tape with butterfly fingers. She would replace the dressing after the doctor left.

I had a blurry memory of a voice from one of the nurses who checked often on me during the night. "Do you have pain in your left shoulder?" she had asked. At that half-awake moment, all I felt was the need to return to a deep sleep. I didn't want to try to listen. "You will have pain in your shoulder, Ellen, when you wake up in the morning," she said too loudly, as if I couldn't hear. "Do not let it worry you, it is because of the gas the doctor used to inflate your abdomen."

I raised my knees now under the covers and scooted back so I was upright against the pillows behind me. I was stabbed suddenly by such an intense pain right under my left shoulder bone that I lost my breath. My eyes teared instantly from the deep burning, cramping agony. My hand whipped up to cover the soft place under my collarbone and I jolted forward, my stomach muscles now convulsing.

"Something is wrong," I heard a faraway voice say. It was my own voice.

"Your shoulder pain is from the gases we used internally during your surgery to inflate the abdomen," Dr. Gomel said, his hand on my back now, as I had folded myself in half over my knees. In crumpling over so reflexively, I had also managed to ignite a different kind of searing pain from my incision. "Try to sit back up slowly. Here you go. You will feel this gas pain for just a day or two and then it will dissipate. I am so sorry. Don't worry, the pain is uncomfortable, but completely normal." I now dimly recalled the nurse's voice during the night.

He guided me back into a sitting position, a third nurse assisting on my other side. I could only take small breaths in an attempt to avoid the pain. "Okay, I am fine now, I was just surprised," I softly reassured everyone around me. I wasn't okay, and I wasn't just fine. I had a killer pain that gripped me each time I took even a shallow breath; but I would never let any of this team of people who were trying so hard to help me have a baby think they had caused this agony. I did not want Peter to see anything from me but a smile. I didn't want him to worry about me, nor could I risk him regretting going along with this quest that had brought us to Vancouver, to this hospital, to this pain.

Late that afternoon I awoke to Peter's words as he stepped into my room.

"Happy Thanksgiving!" He presented me with a white paper bag and laid an identical bag on his chair next to my bed. Inside I found a turkey sandwich on white bread with two squeeze-packets of mayonnaise, a bag of Ruffles potato chips, a napkin, a plastic knife, and a giant sugar cookie. "You can't believe the challenge I had trying to find turkey for us! It isn't Thanksgiving in Canada, so I couldn't find a take-out turkey dinner anywhere. I tried three different restaurants until settling for a deli that had turkey sandwiches."

"Cheers! We have a lot to be thankful for this year," he toasted me with a red can of Coke.

It was with shared smiles that we ate our sandwiches—feeling so hopeful, thankful, and excited to go home and start our family. We had no idea that evening how many more Thanksgiving dinners Peter would share with me in hospitals in the years to come.

The Father of Microsurgery

Dr. Gomel performed microsurgery on me in 1979. Microsurgery is a technique where the surgeon operates using long-handled, delicate instruments viewed under the magnification of a microscope. To perform microsurgery on Fallopian tubes, the scope and operating tools are inserted into the patient through an incision in the woman's navel.

Dr. Victor Gomel was a pioneer using microsurgery on Fallopian tubes in the 1970s. He was the first surgeon in Canada to use microsurgery and is revered in the country as "the Father of Microsurgery." He is internationally acclaimed for his innovative gynecological surgery pioneering both laparoscopy and microsurgery. Dr. Gomel is Professor Emeritus and was a fifteen-year chairperson of the University of British Columbia Department of Obstetrics and Gynecology. He famously founded an in vitro fertilization program that achieved the birth, in October 1983, of Canada's first test-tube baby. He is the author of numerous articles in international scientific and medical journals and has authored several books. In 2003 President Jacques Chirac of France honored Dr. Gomel with the National Order of the Legion of Honour. In 2008 he was elected Fellow to the World Academy of Art and Science. He has been honored with awards of excellence and honorary degrees from multiple international universities.

I was incredibly fortunate to find this brilliant physician and to be accepted into his experimental microsurgical program in 1979.

Chapter 5

I was humming the song "Free Bird" as I skied in long, smooth turns down a cruiser run at the end of the day. I felt like a ballerina or an ice-skater gliding so strongly and smoothly. Each time I ski, I always choose one special song to syncopate a rhythm between my brain and body. Yesterday I sang "Brown Eyed Girl" by Van Morrison to myself. Now I was enjoying Lynyrd Skynyrd as I swished across the groomed slope. The afternoon sun threw a dark purple shadow of my motion on the snow in front of me. The sun had been brilliant all day and the sky was "Crested Butte blue," a color I have never seen anywhere else in the world but above this mountain. Peter and I had spent the morning on the back side of the mountain, commenting on the striated rocks of Aspen's

Maroon Bells in the distance, and practically dancing through the champagne powder, a surprise gift from an overnight breath of dry winter snow.

None of the other skiers I passed noticed that I was now quietly singing out loud, as each was focusing on their own thoughts while gently carving turns in the snow. "Free Bird" was not just my ski song of the day. Today, it was the lullaby I was softly singing to my baby. I was sure I was pregnant.

I was two days late, and my period was never late. I was positive that Dr. Gomel had been successful with the microsurgery in Vancouver. It was now just over four months later. I dared not even whisper my hopeful excitement to anyone, especially Peter, until I was sure. He knew how optimistic I was about getting pregnant soon after the surgery in Vancouver, and I saw in his face that my bright certainty worried him. "Hope for the best but expect the worst," he'd said.

The past two days had been exhilarating for me alone. I liked that. I knew I had to wait for two weeks after my missed period before going to the doctor for a valid pregnancy test. I would not give Peter even a hint until I was absolutely sure. I couldn't put him in limbo, possibly ending with disappointment. He would be more upset for my dashed hope than for himself. Besides, skiing now with my baby and singing to him was an intimate, private time. Everything felt like a Louis Armstrong "Wonderful World" to me. I planned to keep the secret inside until I knew it was real.

"I can't wait to teach you how to ski, Baby Casey. This is your first time on the slopes and no one else even knows." I sent elated thoughts directly to my baby. I listened to the sound of my skis cutting the snow with a crisp, metallic sound as I made smooth S-turns on my way down to the base of Crested Butte Mountain. The sound was confident and exhilarating, exactly the way my secret percolated inside of me.

. . .

"This is Ellen Casey," I said, with my heart beating so hard I could hear it echo off the walls as I sat in the closed phone booth at my school. "Could you please check to see if the lab has sent up the results of my pregnancy test yet?" It was now two weeks after my missed period.

The phone booth had double accordion doors. I sat in an old wooden chair, my left arm holding the phone to my ear and my left elbow on the little shelf that held a phone book and the phone. As I waited on hold, I looked through the door's windows to the hallway where I had hung bright self-portraits that my kindergarteners painted last Thursday. I watched as the second grade filed past, carrying their lunch boxes, headed to the lunchroom.

"Mrs. Casey? This is Alice, Dr. Smith's nurse. Let me just look in your file." I could hear the crisp sound of papers being flipped over, one at a time. I held my breath so long I felt dizzy before she finally spoke.

"Congratulations, Mrs. Casey, you are pregnant."

That evening I lathered my hands thickly with Irish Spring soap at the sink in our bathroom. Then, I carefully stamped a baby footprint on the mirror with the pinky-finger side of my clenched palm and added five little soapy dots (for baby's toes). I marched the baby footprints up the mirror and wrote in lipstick, "Hi, Daddy!"

My mother had told me that in the 1950s her friends used this trick to announce to their husbands they were pregnant. I finally had the chance to use it.

"I'm going to bed now," I called over the bedroom balcony to where Peter was working at the dining room table just below. I noticed thick snow puffs weighing down needle-covered branches of the large pine, towering so close to the window.

"I'll be right up," he answered, but I didn't hear him move.

I couldn't bear lying in the bed waiting, waiting, waiting. After calling down twice to confirm that he was, actually, going to put away his stock market graphs and come to bed, I finally saw the lights go out downstairs and heard Peter's solid steps coming up the stairs. I closed my eyes. He turned left into our bathroom, where I had left the light on. I could see our rust-colored towels with white monogram hanging on the towel bar as he walked in. I just wanted to shout, "We are going to have a baby!" but waited for him to be surprised. I heard each shoe land in the closet where he tossed them, first one and then the other. I heard the whoosh of his Oxford-cloth shirt as it flew through the closet to the hamper.

I finally padded barefoot in my long-sleeved nightgown across our room toward the light. It was late March and still cold and snowy outside. I leaned against the doorjamb, arms and legs crossed casually, as if for a conversation. He still hadn't noticed the mirror. How could he not notice? Peter smiled at me while standing at the sink in his plaid boxers and white T-shirt, and reached for his green toothbrush.

"Did you want something?" he asked formally with a sidewise grin as he squeezed toothpaste in a fat line onto the bristles. I noticed the long, sinewy muscles in his arms.

"Nope," I answered with an enormous smile that made my muscles ache at the sides of my mouth. He started to brush, leaning in toward the mirror, still not looking up at my artwork.

"Yes!" I exploded, laughing, and pointed to the mirror above him. He stepped back and stood still, looking quizzically at the marks. Then he stepped closer and looked a second time.

"No way. You're pregnant?" He looked shocked, not quite daring to smile.

"Yes! Yes! Yes!" I jumped across the room as he engulfed me in a tight hug. He stepped back and looked at my stomach, not even visible under my nightgown. "I talked to Dr. Smith's nurse today and got the results. I went in for a pregnancy test on Monday after school!"

"You don't look pregnant," he commented, his eyes leveled at my stomach. He set his toothbrush on the counter.

"Really? We're really having a baby?" He was now excited. "Good work, Pierre, what a guy!" he congratulated himself looking in the mirror, raising his arms Popeye-style, to show his muscles. "Ha! What a guy." We both just smiled and shook our heads in amazement. Then we laughed again and shook our heads in disbelief.

"When is the baby due?" Peter asked. "Do you even know yet?"

"Thanksgiving," I answered, hands clasped together on my chest.

Chapter 6

"**M**om?" my voice was thin. "Did you have any spotting when you were pregnant with me?" It was late afternoon, just three weeks after my soapy-footprint announcement, and I had made the long-distance call to my mother in Connecticut after coming straight home from teaching. I needed her desperately.

I had been seeing spots of blood on my underpants each time I went to the bathroom during the day. At 10:30 this morning, my stomach felt a jolt like I had just gulped ice water when I first felt the sudden, unmistakable warmth of a period beginning. I had rushed out of my classroom to the ladies' room.

"Oh, Ellen. No, I didn't have any bleeding. But Granny did, and I know it is common early in a pregnancy. Try not to worry, honey. Why don't you call your doctor and talk to him so you won't spend all night feeling frightened?"

I had already made that call hours ago. Instead of eating lunch today, I sat shivering in the same phone booth in the school hallway where I'd heard the news that I was pregnant.

"Mrs. Casey," Dr. Smith's nurse returned to the phone after going to speak to him. "Dr. Smith said that at this early point in your pregnancy, all we can do is wait. If the bleeding gets heavier or if you see clotting, he will want to talk to you. Those could be signs of miscarriage. Do know, however, that spotting is sometimes normal in the first trimester, so there is no need to panic. Why don't you check with your mother and other female relatives to see if this is a familial occurrence? Good luck and be in touch with us if anything changes. And, Mrs. Casey, if you have severe pain, call us immediately and get to the emergency room."

I could feel a marked slackness in my face in the place where a smile had been since learning I was pregnant. For the rest of the afternoon, I had to force myself to act animated with my busy kindergarteners. I asked my teacher's aide to read aloud for story time, as my voice sounded flat when I spoke. I told no one what was happening. I didn't call Peter, and I didn't walk to the first-grade room where my friend Sarah was teaching. This was suddenly only me, alone in my body, and chilled to the bone with private fear for my baby. Five minutes after the children had gone home, I walked through the side door without signing out in the front office. I got in my car and drove straight home. It felt as if weights were clipped to the corners of my mouth, pulling them down.

The yellow phone receiver clattered loudly as I laid it back onto the cradle unevenly, tangling the coiled cord. I jiggled it into place without looking. My mom's voice, tight with hurt for me, doubled my rising fear. I was choking on the agony of daring myself not to face the reality of the disaster that I knew was indeed real. I knew very well that bleeding during pregnancy was not normal. I didn't close my eyes that were blurred with tears. I pushed my breath deep into my diaphragm, willing my mind to close, to stop thinking, and my lungs to stop breathing. I knew it was over. My baby was leaving me drop by drop.

I didn't even have to go in to see Dr. Smith. Friday on the phone he told me that the bleeding I described had most likely been a miscarriage so early in my pregnancy that nothing needed to be done medically. The bleeding had been light and had now stopped. It was either over or it wasn't. I was either still pregnant, he said matter-of-factly, or I wasn't. I just had to wait in dread for two more weeks until a second pregnancy test would be able to tell if I was still pregnant. I wanted to go in to be examined by Dr. Smith, but he said there was no point. Another urine test right now would just show the same pregnancy hormones, and there was no more advanced blood test available. This was why couples didn't announce a pregnancy until after the first three months, when the danger zone for miscarriage had passed.

It seemed like this was nothing but a wait-and-see situation to those closest to me, except for my mom. Nothing? This was my baby. My real baby to whom I sang as we skied in Crested Butte. I was sure it was a baby boy. I had already ordered a soft denim jumpsuit in size newborn from the Wooden Soldier children's catalogue for him. My baby was either gone or still there, the doctor said.

Meanwhile, the baby I wanted for us so badly was floating in limbo in everyone else's mind. Only my doctor, my mom, my good friend Sarah, and Peter knew I was even pregnant. They were the "everyone else."

Peter was sorry, he said, that I was so worried. "But," he assured me, "we now know you can get pregnant after the Vancouver surgery." It had obviously been successful, so we would just "try again if this one doesn't work out," he said. I couldn't even comprehend referring to my pregnancy in such remote terms and stared at him mutely. He seemed distant in choosing to view our situation analytically, as either black or white. I wondered if this was just his reserved demeanor, his non-emotional personality, or if instead he didn't want to deal with how upset he knew I actually was inside.

I felt like I was alone, being bashed by wild waves in a black ocean, and all I could manage was to try to stay afloat. I could count on no one to save me. Not Peter, not the doctor. All I could do was try to stay alive in the midst of this tempest.

My mom called every day to talk to me, confident that I'd just had spotting. She spoke of the Swedish cribs and layettes she had seen at a baby store in New Canaan, Connecticut, where she lived, and helped me stay positively focused on the pregnancy we both prayed I was still carrying. Her calls always left me crying, as I couldn't bear how much she loved me and how much she was trying to help me get through this waiting time, time over which I had no control at all.

"Ellen," she said, "keep smiling. You are the most positive person I know and you have to believe that you are pregnant. With your willpower you will keep that pregnancy no matter what! Have Peter take you out to dinner tonight."

Sarah said that as long as there had been no clots, it must not have been a miscarriage. That helped. And Dr. Smith said I had to wait. To the three of them, it seemed, the two-week waiting time stretched into the future and we'd deal with the answer when it arrived. To me, each breath was a prayer that I could hold on to my baby.

After a few more days, I still felt pregnant, and the dread slowly drained from my tight face. My breasts were tender; I was overwhelmed with a heavy need to sleep. I knew these were signs I was still pregnant. Peter and I drove to Vail the following Friday afternoon to spend the weekend. I could go in for another pregnancy test if I wanted to on Tuesday, but it seemed unnecessary as every sign showed our baby was just fine. And it seemed too sad, too risky, to admit out loud to a technician that I could have had a miscarriage.

I had made the decision not to ski. I was not going to put my body at risk. I remembered a crash I had in Copper Mountain earlier that ski season after I caught an edge trying to keep up with Peter. I hit the snow so hard it briefly paralyzed my diaphragm, and I was terrified. I was afraid to tell Peter I didn't want to ski today. I knew that things had completely changed for me now, but I also didn't want him to think this pregnancy was a disruption to our life. I needed everything about our baby to feel positive to him. It was like I was in a negotiation between a baby and its father, wanting both to win. My stomach was nervous, but I told him my decision as we got out of the car in the parking lot nearest the ticket booth.

"Really?" He looked at me, disappointed, goggles already on his head. I was letting him down. "Come on, you always ski. Put on your boots." Did he think I was no longer going to be fun?

I explained very seriously that I was not about to jeopardize our baby by falling today, on the last day of this year's ski season. I walked to the lift with him and said good-bye. I didn't feel like myself at all as I watched him walk away carrying his skis and then stopping to buckle up his bindings. He didn't look back but poled right over to get in the lift line. I felt like a loser, a non-athlete, a failure in my husband's eyes.

Peter had always complimented me on "keeping up with the boys." Ever since college, my friends and I had always laughed among ourselves in a self-congratulatory way at the fair-weather skiers who shopped and lunched in the ski towns while we, the hard-core, skied the entire day. It was startling that today I was one of the lightweights. Still, the protective feeling for my baby was totally overwhelming, and for the first time in my life, I walked around a ski town while my husband skied without me. When I met Peter at the bottom of the lift at 4 PM, he had a spring sunburn and was gloriously exhausted. I had a small blue teddy bear in a bag from Gorsuch dangling from my hand.

• • •

A week later, I had my foot on the black leather dashboard and was focusing on the rope sandal that flipped on and off my heel when I moved my toes. It was a surprisingly warm April day. Peter smoothly steered our red Porsche Targa through the tight curves on Ute Pass as we wound down toward town. We had leased the brand-new car from the dealer less than a month after our January 13th wedding just last year, euphoric with the enormous, insane power of new love.

A Bob Seger tape was playing in the cassette player and I hummed along. The spring snow thaw higher in the Rockies caused Fountain Creek, running just below us down the middle of the Pass, to be too full and rushing dangerously fast. I had caught a glimpse of it seconds earlier, running turbulent and frothy. I shuddered with a soupçon of dread from memories of rafting through ferocious rapids several summers earlier in Idaho and Utah. Even though my friends guiding us through those rapids had been experts, I never felt completely safe.

Suddenly, I gasped sharply as I was momentarily blinded by white lightning. A shocking pain seared through the soft part of my lower-left side between my hip bone and navel. It felt like a red-hot poker was pressed against me.

"Oh my God," I tried to say out loud, but instead I heard agony squeeze my voice into a sound like a small animal screeching softly, so tiny that Bob Seger's voice drowned mine out completely. When I could catch a new breath, I hunched down, pressing my palms onto my lower abdomen and pushing as hard as I could; I was trying to hold the pain in place. It felt like some horror was going to shoot right out of me if I released the pressure one iota.

"Peter," I winced over the music. "Something is wrong. I'm dying. This hurts so much I really can't stand it." My head felt light and my fingertips were tingly.

"What?" He was surprised and looked over, then down, to see if what he had heard me say was real. "What's wrong? Is something wrong?" He paused. "Wait. Are you all right?"

I felt stunningly calm. I felt both still and icy, analytical and physical. It was as if I were suspended in time and space, with my brain and body working with and against each other. While I physically pressed into my pain, I knew definitively what was happening from the studying I had done during the past five weeks.

I had read every chapter in every book on early pregnancy complications in our downtown Pikes Peak Library. My spotting weeks ago had fired me into academic research mode, one in which I felt very comfortable. From age six to graduation at eighteen, I had thrived in my beloved school, Laurel School for Girls, in Shaker Heights, Ohio. I continued on to Colorado College for both my BA and master's degrees. Taking notes in the library this month had centered me. I knew I had the facts I needed to assess what was happening in my now eight-weeks-pregnant body. A second pregnancy test had shown I was still pregnant, but intellectually I knew I was still in that precarious first three months.

"I am having an ectopic pregnancy," I whispered to Peter. "The baby is growing in my Fallopian tube, which is now bursting—and I could die."

"*What?*" Still driving, he wasn't looking at me. His question hung in disbelief, as though he was trying to analyze what I'd just said. "Shall I stop at the 7-Eleven in Manitou and call your doctor from the pay phone?"

"No, we have to get to the emergency room. This is killing me." I grimaced and rocked my body slightly up and down in the car seat. "If the tube bursts, I will start hemorrhaging internally and it is really dangerous. Really, really, dangerous." I heard myself groan from deep in my throat.

A few seconds passed with the silence broken only by Bob Seger's gravelly voice.

"Peter, this is really important. If I pass out, that means the tube has burst and I am going into shock. You have to keep driving no matter what. Do not stop for anything. Promise me? I mean it, you have to promise that no matter what happens with me right now, you will keep driving to the hospital."

Silence.

"Do you promise?" My voice was desperate with pain and knowledge.

"Okay, okay." I knew Peter was doing the best he could to digest this information. "Good thing we have a sports car," he joked without smiling.

• • •

I knew we were at the hospital. I had consciously forced myself to stay awake long enough to get there and to tell the intense person with a clipboard walking quickly next to my moving bed that I was eight weeks pregnant, that this was an ectopic, I was sure, and that my doctor was Dr. Smith. Now I was finished. Peter could tell them the rest. I was going to go to sleep. It was all I could do. I had to go to sleep.

Someone sat me up and helped me put my arm through a sleeve on a gown. I was aware I was in a room now. Peter was holding my shoulders from behind so I wouldn't fall off the bed. I felt limp. I stared at a face looking at me with big dark-circled eyes; it was my face in the mirror over the sink, but the color was all wrong. I was glow-in-the-dark green, luminescent with black holes where my eyes sat, and my expression was strange. I lay back down with someone's help and surrendered into sleep, sleep, sleep. That was all I wanted.

"Her blood pressure is dropping. Tilt her bed up to see if I can get a blood pressure. Ellen? Ellen? Ellen?" It was a nurse, using a startling voice on purpose, but I didn't want to answer. I was not going to answer. I heard a whirring noise and felt my legs moving up into a steep angle as my bed tilted. My head was going down, down, down. The pain got violently intense, then completely stopped.

"Ellen, Ellen, look at me. Look at me!" It was Peter calling from somewhere far away. "Open your eyes and look at me!" I worked hard to flutter my eyes open just enough to glimpse his face.

"Dr. John Smith, report to Surgery Room IV stat. Dr. John Smith, report to Surgery IV stat."

I heard the announcements in the distance, but I was so far away. So—far—away. Gone.

• • •

I awoke to Colorado mountain quiet. It was that precious moment before being conscious, the sweet, innocent seconds before the sudden jolt startled my sleeping mind with terror. Shock waves alerted me that there had been a disaster. What was wrong? What was dreadfully wrong?

I rolled slightly to my right side, resisting the question, and winced from the wound stretching completely across my abdomen, hip bone to hip bone. There was a crinkly sounding plastic cover over a huge, gauze bandage that covered much of my torso. My body and my mind were suddenly synchronized in abject anguish.

I was home from the hospital. I'd had emergency surgery. Our baby was forever gone.

My eyes were closed, but I was awake. It was my first morning back at home. I remembered everything, all at once, and was grateful that I did not have to spend a fourth night in that hospital room. Our king-sized bed was silent next to me, and I didn't want to open my eyes to confirm I was alone. Peter had already left for work. The New York Stock Exchange opening bell rings at 7 AM Colorado time, and he was always at his desk an hour before then.

Three days ago I had a future. I had plans. I was ecstatic that our baby was due just weeks before Thanksgiving. My mom would be here from Connecticut. I pictured us passing the baby back and forth as we cooked the turkey. My mom would wear an apron and insist that I do, too. Peter would watch college football until dressing for dinner. It was so real that I could even smell the turkey and see our table set with my grandmother's Ginori china and her monogrammed sterling. Our wedding crystal would sparkle in the dinner candlelight.

Three days ago I had worked on a list of my favorite children's books to order from Chinook Bookshop. Peter and I had been headed down the Pass to the bookstore when the first pain hit. It was as if an earthquake had knocked me completely off my foundation, and this morning my life lay shattered in shards around me. Just three days ago I was a completely different woman. Today, I was empty. Everything lay ruined at my feet. My baby, our little family's future, and every bit of hope had broken into irreparable pieces.

My only plan now was to never get out of bed again.

Ectopic Pregnancy Facts and History of Treatment

In April 1980, I was well aware that my life was very much at risk with an ectopic pregnancy, that risk highly increased, in my case, with a ruptured tube. Ectopic pregnancy occurs when the fertilized egg implants somewhere other than the mother's uterus. In more than 95 percent of cases, this occurs inside the Fallopian tube, which is why this condition is often referred to as a tubal pregnancy.

One of the major risk factors for this condition is pelvic inflammatory disease, caused in me by the IUD. Another is tubal surgery, which can leave scar tissue on which a fertilized egg can get stuck as it travels down the tube to the uterus. Tubal pregnancy can occur from earliest pregnancy to 10 to 12 weeks. Mine ruptured at 8 weeks.

In 1980 the only available treatment for an ectopic pregnancy was major surgery to remove the Fallopian tube in which the embryo was growing. This required using general anesthesia and making an incision completely across the mother's abdomen. My ruptured tube was removed during emergency surgery, saving my life.

There was also no easy way to diagnose that the embryo was growing inside the Fallopian tube when I had my ectopic. Mortality rates were 1.15 deaths per 100,000[1] at this time, so early detection and treatment became imperative for obstetric physicians, radiologists, and chemists to

---

1   Andreea A. Creanga, Carrie K. Shapiro-Mendoza, et al., "Trends in Ectopic Pregnancy Mortality in the United States: 1980–2007," *Obstetrics and Gynecology*, 2011: 837–43.

explore. Ultrasound was not specific enough to see a microscopic embryo developing inside the tube. It was not yet known that blood tests showing a lower-than-normal level of the pregnancy hormone, hCG, were an early indicator of tubal pregnancy.

Ectopic pregnancy had long been a major cause of death in women. It was in 1883 when Dr. Robert Lawson Tait, a British surgeon, was the earliest known to save a woman from dying as the result of a ruptured, or close to rupturing, tubal pregnancy. He was distressed that 60 percent of women died as a result of burst Fallopian tubes. He began to operate on women, with the goal to save the patient by removing the ruptured tube. He was very successful. Of his first forty-four patients, forty-two survived what would have been certain death without his surgical intervention. Nearly one hundred years later, it was Lawson's early work that saved my life, as doctors in 1980 routinely surgically intervened in tubal pregnancies.

Presently, there are precise methods to diagnose ectopic pregnancy early. When stabbing pain and bleeding or other known risk factors, such as previous PID, tubal surgery, induced abortions, or a history of smoking, are present, doctors know to look for early indications of trouble. There are now specific, early drug interventions that result in blocking further embryonic cell growth. A drug called Methotrexate is a treatment that stops the growth of an embryo implanted in a Fallopian tube, thus negating the need for emergency surgery and tubal ligation or removal. Today, deaths from ectopic pregnancy have declined significantly.

Chapter 7

On the guest bed above me lay a medium-sized padded envelope. A crumpled sheet of blue tissue paper had fallen from the bed onto the floor. Next to the envelope lay a tiny blue-denim infant onesie. I had forgotten I'd even ordered it, and when the UPS man rang the doorbell, I didn't notice the return address from the Wooden Soldier. I took the package from him, turned in to the guest bedroom, and opened it expectantly on the bed.

My involuntary wail so surprised me that at first I didn't register that it had come from deep within me. The little footed suit was so soft and heartbreakingly dear that when I clutched it to my chest, I couldn't bear it. The sound I released flew up into the air, as if it was a living thing, and hovered over me.

I sat on the floor wedged between the wall and the four-poster bed, sobbing into my jeans, arms wrapped tightly around my legs. I was alone in the house but tried to sob quietly anyway. When I had wailed my grief aloud, the echo horrified me with its raw intensity. The sound seemed to amplify as it ricocheted off the walls. I leaned back and slid down the wall into this corner. I was frightened by the depth of my impossible loss and the grief that settled into every cell of my body. My chest, arms, eyes, all of me actually ached. I felt like I had as a six-year-old child when I fell off a swing and landed shockingly hard on the ground. My breath was knocked out of my chest, my diaphragm paralyzed. I wondered then—and did again now—if I was going to die.

Once when I was driving from Colorado to Chicago, I saw the aftermath of a terrible car wreck on the opposite side of the highway. I will never forget the sight of an open suitcase that had flown out of the car. It was lying in the summer grass, and carefully folded clothes lay spilled out next to it. I saw the packer's hopeful plans for her family's trip in those neat stacks of T-shirts and shorts, now just lying there. The ambulance had long gone, and no sign of the people who had been riding in the front and back seats, looking out at the wheat-colored fields, thinking their own thoughts before impact, was left. I saw small pairs of shoes and knew there had been children. I hoped that someone would pick up the clothes and place them gently back into that suitcase, brushing off any stray blades of grass.

I wiggled myself out from behind the bed, clutching the bedspread to pull myself up like an invalid. I picked up the newborn suit, carefully folded it, and wrapped it in the tissue paper. I smoothed away wrinkles in the tissue and placed the small bundle into my antique trunk that sat on the floor behind me.

Unstoppable

Later, I sat in a wing chair in the living room looking across at the mountains and trees on the other side of the Pass. The sun poured in through the large windows across the back of our house. It was so beautiful here, high on the mountainside, like being in an airplane. But I felt nothing. My eyes seemed unable to telegraph the neurological signal of recognition of such immense beauty to my brain. I stared blankly. The colors of the clear sky, the crystal sparkles in pink granite outcroppings, the shades of browns, yellows, and greens of the grasses, towering trees heavy with pine cones—none of it registered in my conscious mind. I was in a state of numbness, disconnected from everything around me.

As a little girl I would stand solemnly in Lake Michigan, ankle deep, testing for an undertow. My cousins lined up next to me, and we stared down to see if our feet sank into the sand as each wave pulled back from the shore. Our great-grandfather had drowned in the lake before any of us was born, and our mothers wrapped warnings of the lethal power of an undertow around us like a towel each time we arrived at the beach. The icy water made me aware of each separate bone in my tanned feet, each delineated by the unbearable chill. I would never forget that agony in my tiny feet, nor would I ever forget the depth of the anguish that now had settled into every bone in my body. My baby's absence was a constant presence, continuously rolling like waves on the lake. My body ached for him.

I did not want to go back to work and felt absolutely no guilt or sense of responsibility. I called the school secretary every afternoon and asked her to keep the substitute for one more day. This daily routine had now been going on for three weeks following my ectopic. The doctor had cleared me to return to my kindergarten classroom a full week ago, but I couldn't do it. I wasn't sure I would ever leave our house again.

The phone in the living room rang. I wished I knew whose voice I would hear when I answered. I had had so many calls, some surprisingly sweet and some I wished I hadn't answered at all. A current student's mother had called to say she'd lost her first baby through miscarriage. I hardly knew this woman. Yet she described how she had cried and cried for so many days that her husband threatened to take her back to the hospital to see a psychiatrist. She said that she wouldn't have lunch or even go for a walk with her friends, as seeing people pushing strollers snapped her heart every time. They were everywhere, she remembered, strollers. Then told me she completely understood how I felt, but added that her son, Andrew, missed me, and she hoped I would return to my classroom soon.

The phone rang again. I had to answer it, I knew I did. If it was my mom or Peter and they couldn't reach me, it would cause more worry for them, and each was seriously concerned about me already. "Hello?" I said softly.

"Hi, Ellen, it's Janis," a familiar low voice said. I liked Janis. She was my teammate in the kindergarten classroom next door to mine. She lived in Green Mountain Falls, just up the Pass from us, so our house was on her way home. "I have something from your students to drop off for you," she said. "I promise I won't stay long. Okay?"

I wished I had just let the phone ring and ring. I wanted to scream, "No! I don't want to see you. I don't want to see anyone. I don't want to ever leave my house, and I don't want to see anyone who will remind me that I have responsibilities at work." I only wanted to hide quietly, alone in my house. "Okay," I replied. "I'll see you this afternoon. Thanks, Janis." I had to let her come so that she could tell my students she had delivered their messages to me. I couldn't hurt their feelings, so I forced myself to acquiesce to her visit.

The mountain above us blocked the late-day sun and our house was heavy in blue shadow. I was drifting around the living room, looking at the magazines, mail, and papers that needed to be picked up, sorted, or tossed away. I thought about it, but didn't make a move to organize them. The doorbell rang and I jumped, making my stomach hurt in the empty place below my navel. I did not want to see anyone. I did not want to smile. I did not want to be pleasant.

"Hi, Janis," I said as I opened the door. I wasn't sure if I was smiling or not. I was trying to. She stood there with a large yellow shelf-paper folder, the kind teachers staple together to hold students' work. "Come in."

"Your little guys made cards for you and they are hilarious!" she laughed. She walked in and laid the huge envelope on the dining room table. "How are you?" she asked, turning back to me, and I saw a slight shadow of sympathy pass across her eyes.

"Okay," I lied. I knew that no one wanted to hear me say crushed, or devastated, or I can't imagine how I can live another day. "Okay," I repeated, staring down at the carpet.

"Well, I promised I wouldn't stay and I have to get home before Chris does because I swore that I would make dinner tonight." Janis, who hated to cook, moved sideways toward the front door.

"Oh, wait," she said as she stopped, reached into the backpack slung over one shoulder, and pulled out a white bakery bag. "This is from Cameron in your class. He turned six today and was so sad you weren't there to sing the birthday song. He got really excited when I said I was going to see you tonight, so here is his birthday treat! Lucky you," she joked.

I did smile for real this time as I took the bag, peeked in, and saw the Dixie cup filled with cake and chocolate pudding, topped with gummy worms lying on finely crumbled Oreo cookies. It was a dirt cake, and I knew Cameron had been just beside himself with pride today when he passed them out to his buddies in kindergarten as they all sat expectantly on the floor in a circle. He probably hoped the girls would scream and think the worms were real. They probably did scream, but just for effect, as five-year-old girls love to do.

Janis left. I was grateful she hadn't asked when I planned on returning to work. I tossed the cake into the sink, where the disposal would devour it. Kindergarteners often impulsively licked the icing on the birthday treats their moms made for the class—too much of a temptation. I'd noticed an indentation in the frosting where a gummy worm had been. I chuckled about the missing worm and went to open the envelope. It was full of phonetically spelled cards bearing the messages "We miss you" and "Get well soon," written with crayon on manila paper. I could tell whose card was whose before even reading their names. I knew each little one so well after eight months of teaching them daily. Almost every card had a picture of me with an upside-down U for a mouth, looking tragic. I was usually surrounded in the drawings by flowers, lots and lots of bright, waxy flowers. I sat down and looked carefully at each one. Janis was right, they were hilarious.

I realized it was the first time I had laughed in weeks. I missed being with children. There was no way to maintain being sad around children. The next day I called the school secretary and said I would be back in my classroom on Monday. I would just have to force myself to go. I needed those round faces with missing teeth in their smiles. I missed the hugs around my legs and the knock-knock jokes. I missed daily show-and-tell and noticing T-shirts that had been put on inside out in the morning rush to get to school on time. I missed primary colors.

I missed being happy.

I picked up the stack of cards and went through them again. When I looked at the cards, I actually forgot myself for just a moment. Being with children washed me in the intensity of the feeling of full sun on my back.

I was ready. I suspected that I was still here somewhere underneath this black weight of loss. I would go back to teaching and spend my days with the children I adored. Children were the air I lived in, and I needed to breathe again to survive. In a warm rush, I felt blood flush my pale cheeks. I would never get over this baby, my child. I had loved and had lost him, but I would go back to work.

A week later, I pushed down on the long metal bar and opened my classroom door to twenty-six kindergarteners waiting outside. They were loosely lined up against the brick wall with their backpacks and papers. Each child was in motion. Some had their backs to me; some were looking in another direction shouting to friends. I had forgotten how loud they were. I really didn't want to make eye contact with their parents but smiled and waved one hand at them as if all was just fine. I struggled to stand under the enormous hugs being given around my waist by my little ones as they passed by me on their way into the building. I felt embarrassed and selfish to have been away from my class for so long and, on a strange level, ashamed at having lost my baby in front of these parents. I smiled reassuringly again and closed the door behind me.

It was so easy to get right back into my kindergarten routine of starting each day with the "Good Morning to You" song, then moving to my small chair in front of the calendar and emceeing show-and-tell. The time flew by and I didn't have a free moment to think about my loss. I avoided the front office, the faculty lounge, and being in the hallways. I did not want to see or talk to anyone and felt furtive as I peeked around my door to see if I would be alone in the hall before venturing out to pick up my kids at gym.

When I had no choice but to go to the open-concept library for the week's stack of read-aloud books, I felt naked and vulnerable to assault by well-meaning colleagues. All of the classrooms were arranged with doorways opening into the library, and a constant stream of students, teachers, and parents passed through. I bent down and looked for the section of "K" authors, as I planned to read Ezra Jack Keats books every day that week.

"Ellen, I am so sorry," a fourth-grade teacher said as she stopped her line of students to dart over and hug me at the bookcase where I now held *The Snowy Day*. That sentence would be repeated in many different words by many school staff members and was usually followed by their quick escape. I noticed the relief pass across their faces and saw their bodies relax slightly after each person had expressed sympathy and turned away. Each had made the effort to face me in my grief, and I knew that was hard to do. I did. I also understood the reason they changed the subject and walked off. The very personal human gratitude when a terrible loss belongs to another and your own life remains safe is universal.

I jumped back imperceptibly when someone said, "It was God's will." That was the worst. I felt doused with ice water when I was told "You will get pregnant again right away," as I knew that was impossible. Still, I was grateful to each person who asked how I was for one specific reason: their compassion acknowledged that I did once carry an actual baby and I wanted my lost baby to be mentioned. I needed to hear others give voice to the fact that my baby had been real. It helped me to not feel crazy.

For a week I walked through the school as if I were in a play, an actor whose role was to look normal and put others at ease. My life had been indescribably fractured and I felt as if I were walking and talking underwater. Yet, as the days passed, I began to no longer avoid people but to genuinely welcome their sympathetic acknowledgment in any manner they tried to show it.

It was May now and children were arriving to school in shorts, carrying bouquets of yellow daffodils wrapped in tinfoil. Excitement for summer break was growing, voices were sounding happier, and I, too, was feeling a small hopeful spot inside myself again. I was aware that I had a choice. I could give up and fold inward or I could get back to work and find out how to get pregnant again. I could continue sleepwalking through my days in mourning or open my eyes and search for solutions. I started to recruit every friend to tell me if she had heard of a path we could use to adopt a baby. I asked my friends who didn't work to watch

The Phil Donahue Show and *The Today Show* and take notes for me if anything about infertility was on. I made an appointment with Dr. Smith to discuss what new treatments were available, which doctors were doing experimental trials, and where I could study the newest research for myself. I had an indelible certainty that somehow, Peter and I would have our baby.

I always had a goal. Daddy had taught me to "follow through" when playing tennis and pitching a softball. I watched him experiment as a pioneer in plastics in the 1950s. He had an idea to create a resin in which he could set marble slices to create floor tiles, tabletops, and counters. Mother and I would walk into the house and cup our hands over our noses and mouths in reaction to the overpowering smell of epoxy being cooked in our kitchen oven. Mother was always furious. Some resins solidified into successes and some were dripping failures. I watched as Daddy followed through, never gave in to defeat, and saw his invention become a patented success, which he franchised nationwide. I had been raised to "follow through." It was in my DNA.

Having a baby was the goal of my life.

Surviving the Loss of a Pregnancy

In the early 1980s, doctors were not trained to help their patients deal with the traumatic psychological and emotional effects that followed an ectopic pregnancy or a miscarriage.

My doctors were kind and sympathetic, but I don't remember ever talking about how devastated I was emotionally. My physical healing was carefully watched, but the fact that I had just nearly lost my life as a result of a ruptured Fallopian tube was never mentioned. I was alone to handle my anguish.

Today, the internet has hundreds of sites: blogs, Facebook pages, chat rooms, and resources for mothers and fathers to help them navigate through the physical, psychological, and emotional aftermath of the loss of a pregnancy. Losing a much-wanted baby is devastating; it is painfully difficult to move forward. Acute, paralyzing sadness is to be expected, as are feelings of panic, fear, and extreme vulnerability. The loss of control over her body and fertility following an emergency ectopic or miscarriage is disorienting and threatening to a woman.

Today I know that my agoraphobic feelings and actions were completely normal. But back then, I felt like I was a crazy person when I left a full grocery cart inside of King Soopers one afternoon and ran outside to my car after seeing a woman I knew. I was embarrassed, ashamed, guilty, and overwhelmed with despair at both our loss and my uncertain future as a mother. Isolation was the safest way for me to cope.

I suffered for weeks. No one was available to tell me that this need for isolation was just temporary. No one assured me I did not have a psychiatric disorder and would one day recover to step back into the world with renewed life and hope for the future.

Medical professionals today are aware that a woman who is agonizing privately in her loss is a woman in danger. Thankfully, doctors now are trained to refer patients to multiple grief-counseling resources.

Chapter 8

Every woman I see is pregnant. Sometimes she is wearing a floral-print maternity dress and standing in line in front of me at Safeway, absentmindedly holding the handle of her grocery cart. Other times she wears jeans and a loose striped top as she passes too close to me in the bookshop and smiles an "excuse me." I see her holding hands with her husband in the pew in front of me at church, giving him an intimate smile. She stands talking with two other mothers outside my classroom window before the bell rings and I push open the door to release my students. Her child runs to her and they walk away down the sidewalk together, heading home. She laughs at her ink smears as she sits next to me in calligraphy class at the Fine Arts Center, she flips through Eagles record albums near me at the Independent Records store.

Sometimes she walks slowly and alone as I drive past. She may look happy, she may look tired, she may look preoccupied. She may wear cute clothes or used clothes, flip-flops or heels. It doesn't matter. I always wish I were her.

And it always feels so unfair in that hollow place under my ribs as I suck in my breath and look away.

Every other pregnant woman seems to have a toddler by the hand or is pushing a wiggly two-year-old swinging his chubby hands over the sides of a stroller. They all seem so casual about their babies. "It was an accident," a mother of one of my kindergarteners explained to me on Monday afternoon as she bent over her protruding belly to pick up her daughter's dropped backpack from the sidewalk. She sounded apologetic, almost embarrassed. "We really only wanted two. But, here comes number three!" she said, while patting her stomach and rolling her eyes. I manage a closed-lip smile.

I was at my friend Cathy's one Saturday morning. We sat on the banquette in her large kitchen, talking quietly and sipping coffee. Outside the kitchen's picture windows, yellow-green leaves had sprouted on every branch, causing the mountains behind to turn blue in contrast. Bald, three-month-old Andrew slept on her chest as she lounged back on the Southwestern-striped pillows behind her. The gentle connection between the two of them made my stomach tighten. It was a living Mary Cassatt painting. I was on the outside, viewing this scene. I couldn't look away.

At 11:15, our friend Julie walked through the garage door into the kitchen. She had Jennifer trailing behind her, wearing an appliqued Florence Eiseman jumper with no blouse under it. Her baby shoulders were so round and vulnerable. I registered in a split second how moved I was by the sight of a baby's shoulders, as I said hello quietly. Julie was wearing five-month-old Christopher on her back and carrying a blue-denim diaper bag. I watched as she deftly unclasped the buckle around her waist and lifted off the baby backpack in one smooth motion.

"He is getting so heavy," she muttered to herself, as she flipped open the pack's metal legs, locked them in place, and stood Christopher, still strapped in, on the floor. She sat on the banquette next to me and reached down to open the diaper bag. Cathy asked if Julie liked that Sierra brand of backpack, as Julie pulled out a plastic baggie of cheese strips and a yellow sippy cup, which she handed to Jennifer. The cup had white ducks marching across it. Jennifer leaned against her mom and sipped with glazed eyes watching Cathy and Andrew. Julie handed the baby some pastel plastic keys on a ring, which he immediately put in his mouth.

My mind traveled away as they discussed umbrella strollers and food mills, Andrew's christening outfit on special order at the Broadmoor's Merry Simmons children's shop, and whether Graco car seats were the best. "When are you going to start the baby on solid foods?"

It was like a club I couldn't join. A secret language I didn't understand. A physical connection so deep that touch was a constant form of communication. I was with my friends, but I was not a part of the group. It was a club of mothers and I was not a member.

A week later my friend Kate sat in my classroom at lunchtime. I was having a tuna fish sandwich at my desk. Kate was sitting in a child-sized chair at one of the long Formica tables, resting her head on her folded arms. I noticed a large chip had been banged off of the table edge.

"I'm pregnant, and I don't want to be pregnant," she moaned. "I am not even sure I want to be married to David anymore." I laid my sandwich down on top of the creased waxed paper in which I had wrapped it that morning.

She lifted her head. "I don't even know if this baby is Dave's or JP's," she practically shouted toward me, then put her head back down on her arms and made another moaning sound.

It was a good thing she couldn't see my face. I was stunned into stillness. I had no idea that she was having an affair with JP, who worked at a popular ski shop in Colorado Springs. She and her husband, David, had met freshman year at college in New Hampshire and had been married immediately when they graduated. David was a darling and was devoted to her. By getting attached to him at eighteen and marrying so very young, Kate had missed her chance to be the flirtatious party girl—dancing on the tables, leaving a trail of men in her wake—she thought she could and should have been.

She had now just apparently confessed to making up for lost time. I took a quick breath, and no reply came out of my lips. I sat paralyzed at my gray metal desk.

"What am I going to do?" came a whine. She did not look at me. "I don't want a baby!"

My immediate reaction was to shriek, "Are you kidding me? Of all the people on this planet, why are you complaining about being pregnant to ME?" This friend had visited me in the hospital after the drastic emergency surgery that removed my only open Fallopian tube. She watched me grieve after I lost our baby. She knew that I could not have a baby naturally now, and she was complaining to me about being pregnant? I felt disbelief. Anger burned my cheeks as I remained silent.

Kate worked at a nonprofit nearby and often stopped in to the school where I taught to have lunch with me. She and I had just spent the weekend before in Aspen, where her family had a condo at the base of the slopes. We raced between and over the snowy moguls together, skiing as well and as fast as we could, perhaps to impress each other. She knew I had gone to Vancouver for surgery. She knew I was desperate to have a baby.

"I had an abortion when we were in college," came the next sentence from her mouth. She was looking right at me.

"What?" I involuntarily gasped. "You never told me."

"We were just freshmen. It wasn't a baby; it was a problem," she stated very firmly. She held my eyes with hers in an unspoken challenge.

"Hmm," I mumbled through my nose. It didn't seem safe to respond on any level at that point.

• • •

I thought back to another conversation, with another good friend, six years earlier.

I remember very clearly when Kirsten was going through sorority rush as a sophomore transfer student to Colorado College. A letter of recommendation was read aloud to the girls sitting on the couches and blue-carpeted floor of our house as we tried to decide which women we might want to invite to be our new sorority sisters. The letter writer related a vivid story, alive with colors, sounds, and smells, of how Kirsten, who was her teenage summer babysitter, had saved her toddler from drowning after the baby fell into a watering trough while the rest of the family was saddling up for a horseback ride.

Kirsten was a music major. We both were student teachers during our senior year and sat on the dorm floor together in the evenings cutting out paper bulletin board decorations. We adored children. After we graduated, Kirsten went to work on a master's in music education in Boulder, and I began teaching five-year-olds in Colorado Springs. She was spending the summer working as a music camp counselor in the mining town of Cripple Creek.

"I am going to be in the Springs for a doctor's appointment at noon Thursday, so let's meet at Michelle's for ice cream afterward!" she said one night in August on the phone.

As I entered the ice cream shop, cowbells hanging from a leather strap on the door rang to announce my arrival. The front room smelled cold and sweet. I walked past the candy counter full of perfectly arranged handmade candies.

The back room beyond the candy displays had gray faux-marble tables in the center and red high-backed booths along the side walls. Double swinging doors flapped at the back, as servers scurried in and out of the kitchen. I chose one of the red vinyl booths. I both felt and heard the cushion puff out air as I plopped down and waited. I fingered the long ice cream spoon the waitress had placed at each setting, looking up toward the door every two or three seconds as I waited for Kirsten. I sipped water from the curvy water glass just to feel busy. I was breathing so quickly I almost felt light-headed. I couldn't stand another second of waiting for my friend.

Then, there she was. Kirsten, my tall Nordic friend, swinging her straight, shoulder-length, champagne-colored hair, pale green eyes under dark brows, her pink cheeks glowing, running toward me. We both started talking at the same time as we sank into opposite seats, hands squeezing each other's tightly across the table. In one sentence I asked about her sisters back home in Minnesota with her parents, and a new grad-school boyfriend whom I hadn't met.

Kirsten lifted my hands, still clenched in hers, off of the table and shook them slightly to stop my talking. "Ellen, I'm pregnant."

I never took my eyes off of hers. "What will you do?" I whispered, as my stomach flip-flopped.

"We are getting married!" she said, eyes shining and a smile covering her whole face. I was surprised, shocked, and a tiny bit jealous far back inside me. Kirsten was going to have a baby. She was going to have what I had always known I wanted, a baby.

"Oh, my God! I am so, so, so happy for you!" I said too loudly for a restaurant full of diners. I didn't care. Kirsten was in love, getting married, and pregnant. We jumped up and met again at the metal edge of our table and hugged and cried. "Kirsten, a baby! A tiny, precious baby! Oh, my God! You're a mom!" We rocked back and forth in a tight embrace, noticing the pair of sixty-year-old ladies smiling at us from the closest table.

How casually and easily Kirsten had conceived.

And now here I was with Kate, again having conceived without even trying—or wanting to get pregnant. It made me feel like a piece of glass was caught in my throat. Guilt and envy choked me.

I turned toward Kate, who repeated, "What am I going to do?"

I was quiet as she continued. "*You* really want a baby, and *I* just want to be free," she said through tears. "I wish I could just give you this one!"

"I wish you could, too," I said after releasing a huge sigh, shaking my head side to side. *I wish you could, too.*

Chapter 9

"My mother says maybe God doesn't want Ellen to have a baby," my neighbor said casually as she leaned against the counter in our kitchen grating cheddar cheese on a late July afternoon.

"What?" I felt like I had been punched in the solar plexus. I had thought about my lost baby every single day since my ectopic three months earlier. I couldn't believe what I had just heard.

I whirled around from the stove, still holding my wooden spoon, poised to shout, "She said what?" My back had been turned to her as I stirred taco meat on the stove and I had only heard her words, not seen her face as she delivered them. I stopped, mid spin, when I saw her expression. My ponytail lashed my cheek, I had turned so fast. She looked up from grating and was starting to laugh.

My wooden spoon now dripped tiny red spots on the floor. I knew that her devout Catholic mother was sad for us that I had lost the baby, so I was shocked at this statement. She had looked at me seriously when she joined her daughter to deliver us dinner after the ectopic pregnancy surgery, frown lines furrowing as she patted my hand and said, "I'm sorry, dear, but you will have others." That was what women said to each other and I knew it had been difficult for her to even bring it up. Miscarriage was simply not discussed. It was 1980, and this was a very private matter.

In the 1950s, I wore white wrist-length gloves to Sunday School and always bobbed in a curtsy when shaking hands with an adult. In the late 1960s, I still stood when an adult entered the room, curtsied to the headmaster of my school at the end of the day, and wore an unmanageable girdle on my seventy-five-pound, fourteen-year-old frame when I was dressed up.

Then I began to hear Vietnam War protest songs on the radio, sung by Bob Dylan and Peter, Paul, and Mary. My friends and I were elated when our private girls' school accepted its very first black students and integration became real in our lives. I laughed as I saw women's liberation protestors toss their bras off of bridges and couldn't wait to get to college so I could wear bell-bottoms like Cher did on *The Sonny and Cher Show*. This was a time of extreme change. Flower children and hippies smoked marijuana on the streets of Haight-Ashbury, the Beatles' long hair was shocking, and yet the social mores among my parents and their friends remained exactly the same. Good manners, good taste, and respecting another's privacy precluded public acknowledgment of any personal situation.

"Maybe God doesn't want Ellen to have a baby."

I wouldn't have been surprised one bit if her mother had said exactly those words. If the suggestion had come from a priest, I imagined she absolutely would have taken his word. The Catholic Church, just like adults our parents' age, hadn't changed at all while the world danced braless around them.

. . .

Peter and I were visiting friends in Aspen in late July 1978, the summer before we got married. We hiked a trail one morning to Maroon Lake through fields of wildflowers. The lake was even more glorious than the jaw-dropping photos I had seen. The water was perfectly still, reflecting a mirror image of the striking Maroon Bells and our brilliant Colorado sky. I felt euphoric with awe and was still smiling when we got back to the house and the news came on the television. The world's first test-tube baby had been born in England. The public was thrilled for baby Louise Brown's parents, yet also stunned by a conception never before expected to become a reality. One of our friends laughed over the broadcast, "Oh, boy, I can hear my mother wondering what the Pope will say about this baby." It was my first glimpse of how powerful the influence of the Roman Catholic Church was going to be in my life.

Several months later, in early December, we were actively planning our wedding; it was going to be in Colorado Springs on January 13, 1979—in just six weeks. Peter waved me in through the glass doors of his office at E. F. Hutton when he saw me arrive on a Friday afternoon. He was on the phone.

As I waited for him to finish his call, I thought back to one year earlier, when I had first glimpsed him through these same doors. I was waiting outside of the office on the Persian carpet in the entry hall. I loved the ornate building, constructed during the Cripple Creek Gold Rush of the 1890s. When the stockbroker I was dating at the time walked through the doors to take me out after work, I casually asked, "Who is that?" motioning my head in the direction of the tan, dark-haired man in a pink shirt and navy-blue sports coat talking on the phone. "Oh, that is the new guy from Boston, Peter Casey," my date answered.

"That's right, Mom," Peter was now saying on the phone, "I said Grace Episcopal Church." I looked at Peter's tight-lipped expression. We had already met with the Episcopal priest and had our wedding planned at the church a few blocks away from the Colorado College campus. It was a replica of Westminster Cathedral. I had first slipped inside the granite sanctuary during my sophomore year to say a prayer the day my darling grandfather died in Chicago.

"Well, we'll miss you then," Peter said. "Bye, Mom." He hung up the phone, looking perturbed but not visibly concerned. "She says she won't come if the service isn't in a Catholic Church." He shook his head and added, "The Catholic Church is important to her. Don't worry one bit. She'll be there. She loves us."

• • •

I looked across the kitchen now toward the counter where my neighbor, who was clearly making a joke and not intending to upset me, had turned sideways to me and was grating cheese again onto our wooden cutting board. Her words, "My mother says maybe God doesn't want Ellen to have a baby," still hung like a stiff, black net, veiling my eyes. I knew I shouldn't take the words personally. Still, the Catholic Church's influence in those words invaded my heart, making my ribs feel bruised. Could she actually believe that if a priest suggested this in counsel, it was true? I wondered if my new mother-in-law, who I so wanted to impress, felt the same way.

When I was ten years old and John F. Kennedy was running for president, his Catholic faith was a huge issue. I overheard adults saying in strong tones that if we had a Catholic president, the Pope would be making decisions for America. At ten, I was both impressed and worried that the Pope could have such power. I could not imagine what he might tell our president that would be disastrous, but if the adults were worried, I was, too.

That summer afternoon in my Rocky Mountain kitchen, I had no idea what was still to come. Three years after our Episcopal wedding, Peter and I were required to be married a second time—in a Roman Catholic Church. The church's social ministry declined to add our names to the list of couples hoping to adopt, because we hadn't been married by a Catholic priest. We even had to take the Pre-Cana (before marriage) course in the evenings. Though I sincerely meant it when I signed my name on a document promising to raise our child as a Catholic if we were successful adopting through the Catholic Church, I wore a red-knit suit to our private wedding ceremony in a wink of defiance.

Nor could I ever have imagined that, a few years following our Catholic wedding ceremony, I would be on live television, my toddler on my lap, responding to Pope John Paul II's official document. He had pronounced, on March 10, 1987, in "Instruction on Respect for Human Life in Its Origins and on the Dignity of Procreation," that in vitro fertilization—the method of my precious baby's conception—was "morally illicit."

I tactfully responded to the newscaster's direct challenge as she raised her eyebrows and asked, "Are you saying the Pope is wrong?"

"Oh, no, I would never say the Pope is wrong, but perhaps misguided, removed. He just doesn't understand the God-given love between a man and woman for himself. He can't possibly know the strength of a husband and wife's desire to have their own biological child." I smiled sweetly at the newscaster, then directly into the camera.

Religion, Marriage, and Infertility Treatment

Life-altering advances in birth control for women, with the release of the birth control pill in 1960, followed by astounding biomedical technology to treat and reverse infertility in the 1980s, threw religious institutions into an ethical turmoil.

Churches attempted to carefully study these scientific methods to facilitate pregnancy, or to prevent it, with the goal of being able to release position statements for their members to follow.

On July 25, 1968, Pope John Paul VI released his encyclical at a Vatican press conference. The pill was proclaimed an artificial method of birth control, making its use by members of the Roman Catholic Church a mortal sin.

Women were finally able to take control of their own reproductive lives and choose when to have, or not have, children. But a Roman Catholic woman now faced a terrible dilemma.

In 1979, Peter—who was raised Catholic—and I were married in my church, the Episcopal Church. I understand now that the Catholic Church considered our marriage invalid, as we did not petition a bishop for permission to marry outside of the Roman Catholic Church. We needed to have an official "Dispensation for Canonical Form" to be allowed to marry outside the Catholic Church.

When I had surgery to open my Fallopian tubes, I was also in violation of the Catholic dogma of natural conception. IVF was condemned by the Catholic Church on February 22, 1987, as the Vatican doctrinal statement concluded the matter this way:

continued

"Nevertheless, in conformity with the traditional doctrine relating to the goods of marriage and the dignity of the person, the Church remains opposed from the moral point of view to homologous 'in vitro' fertilization. Such fertilization is in itself illicit and in opposition to the dignity of procreation and of the conjugal union, even when everything is done to avoid the death of the human embryo."[2]

In vitro fertilization, which would become the means of our child's conception, was "illicit" in the eyes of the Church.

---

2 "Instruction on respect for human life in its origin and on the dignity of procreation: Replies to certain questions of the day," Supreme Pontiff, John Paul II, February 22, 1987. See https://www.vatican.va/roman_curia/congregations/cfaith/documents/rc_con_cfaith_doc_19870222_respect-for-human-life_en.html.

Chapter 10

I am practiced at handling life alone. I am an only child. I never had a brother or sister to huddle with forlornly in pajamas at the top of the stairs and listen, in fear for our future, to our parents arguing in the library far below at night. No one ever knew that I agonized alone about whether my parents would get divorced—an imagined blast that would blow my child's life into a million burning pieces. Nor did I have a sibling to snuggle with on Christmas Eve in excitement or to make secret plans with under the blankets by flashlight. I never leaned on anyone during sad times nor held someone's hand in the good.

I was a junior at Colorado College the spring I got a long-distance call from my mother in California. I sat in the heavy oak phone booth in the front hall of my dorm, holding the black receiver attached to the pay phone, trying to make sense of Mother's words. It was a hideously familiar flashback. My brain was in this exact same shocked state when I was fifteen and heard on a Friday afternoon that President Kennedy had been shot. Now, Mother calmly stated that she had left my father, sold the precious family piano my great-grandfather had brought across the ocean with him from England, and was moving that day from California to Wilmette, Illinois, to live with her father.

She announced coolly, like a footman reading a proclamation from the queen, that there was no money anymore and I would have to drop out of college. I saw myself from afar as a child in a white nightie, standing in an endlessly long hallway on an oriental carpet runner as it was pulled swiftly out from under my feet. In my slow-motion vision, I floated up in the air, spinning, spiraling, somersaulting backward. I floated softly back down and landed on the polished floor. I was standing absolutely still on two bare feet.

I was completely alone.

I walked silently right past my best friend's door. I didn't need sympathy or advice. I needed to make a plan. I entered my dorm room, mind racing, every option examined. I brushed my hair, walked out the door, and straight across the grassy quad to the gray stucco Administration building. I stepped into the open door of the financial aid office and asked to please speak to Mr. Howard, whose name I read on the metal plaque just outside as Director of Financial Aid. I sat in a chair across from him and succinctly described the phone call from Mother.

I had always lived a privileged life of private school, country clubs, ballet classes, equitation lessons, and travel with my parents.

This shocking, life-altering financial catastrophe was absolutely foreign to me. Still, calm confidence took over my body. I sat straight in the chair and resolutely told Mr. Howard I needed his help to stay in school. Surprisingly, I didn't feel shame. Pride was a non-issue. My spine had turned to solid metal. The strength I needed to achieve my goal took over. I had to stay at Colorado College. That was all that mattered to me, and I knew I could—I would—do it. And I did.

I learned that day I alone was the driver of my own life. Having the financial and safe familial rug pulled out from under me was a harsh reality check that tested my character. Difficult as this experience was, it steeled me to navigate all that was to come in my life ahead.

I took that determination to Europe with me two years after graduation, when in 1973, my college friend Evie and I walked off a plane from Chicago into the wildly bustling airport in Rome. We were twenty-three years old. I had the thick paperback *Europe on 5 Dollars a Day* in my bag, so was completely undaunted by our loose plans for a six-country, six-week backpack trip through Europe. I knew where we wanted to go, what I wanted to see, and was excited to handle detours, languages, and the unexpected. Overcoming Evie's terrified look, I navigated through the crowd and got us into an Italian cab and confidently gave the driver instructions to our first destination, a youth hostel.

Back then I had a financial aid officer and a European guidebook to help me reach my goals. But now, in my venture to find a medical way to get pregnant, there was no such guide. It was a solitary situation.

I didn't know even one other woman dealing with infertility whom I could ask for advice, names of doctors, or just for comradery. If other couples were trying and failing to have a baby, Peter and I would never have known. It was 1980 and this personal tragedy was kept private and never discussed. I did hear of friends of friends, a radiologist and his wife, who quietly adopted, but no one knew why they couldn't have a baby of their own.

Infertility was shrouded in a great silence. Perhaps it was shame or guilt or a sadness so deep, so anguished over not being able to get pregnant. I didn't feel that. Fortunately, I never felt a need to have someone in whom to confide or with whom to commiserate. I alone held the power to discover how I would be able to have our baby. I was challenged to be in sole charge of my own outcome. I had intelligence, education, and confidence. I knew how to do research, seeking out primary sources. I was prepared and eager to begin.

• • •

I had no idea that the public library in our hometown of Colorado Springs had a basement. Descending the steep stairs for the first time, I thought of Dante's *Inferno*. It was as if I had taken a wrong turn in a familiar place and ended up mistakenly in an employees-only back room.

The familiar building felt foreign and much older down in the basement. The underground library quiet seemed heavy and oppressive in contrast to the upstairs. No one was even whispering. Upstairs there was soft noise: men talking in low voices to the librarians, mothers whispering sharply to their kids as they hurried toward the Children's Room. Light shone through big windows, and people bent low, looking intently at book spines for the numbers taped on in white. Students sat at tables flipping pages that sounded like sheets of wrapping paper being tucked around presents. People walked from the card catalogue toward the long rows of bookshelves, holding notes on which they had written Dewey Decimal System numbers in pencil. There was constant movement. There was a low hum of sound.

The phones I heard ringing behind the desks upstairs did not ring belowground in the basement. Fluorescent lighting emitted a barely perceptible, high-pitched buzz and created a bright blue-white glare that made me want to squint. The ceilings were low. It was odd down there.

Yet I loved how it felt walking down the institutional stairs that opened into this secret space. As I stood and first looked around this open, strange room, I felt confidence and purpose tighten my lower back muscles, causing me to stand erect. The thrill I felt entering the research floor glistened with possibility. Awareness of being in complete control of my own life felt immediately familiar. It was like being back in school.

In my condition, the doctors knew I was at a dead end, in a medically impossible state to conceive. I had just turned thirty-one, had one blocked Fallopian tube, and my other tube ruptured and had been removed with the ectopic pregnancy, five weeks earlier. Louise Brown's birth in England in 1978—just two years ago—confirmed that this was a time of stunning, experimental infertility treatments in medicine. I felt my jaw muscles clench as I nodded once, confidently, to myself. I would find the top doctors and scientists attempting the most unique, innovative treatments. I found Dr. Gomel, and was ready to do more research until I found the next doctor who would help me. I would spend all day, every day researching in this library basement. Failure was absolutely not an option. Peter and I *would* have a baby.

"Here are your boxes of microfiche," the librarian said softly one afternoon in the library basement. "Let's go find a free microfilm machine, and I will show you how to load the film." I followed her into a small room about the size of a child's bedroom, where there was a long shelf on which were sitting five unused gray machines.

Flat cardboard boxes I had already used sat stacked on my left, and on my right were the unviewed films—still in boxes, still holding possibilities. I stood to stretch my stiff back and legs and walked to the door for a short break. I had been sitting for four hours.

After bending down to touch my shoes, then reaching my fingers straight into the air, I looked out from the doorway into the large library space. I saw the round table where I'd spent my entire morning. The *Readers' Guide to Periodical Literature* sat on that table and on other tables as well—each as thick as a dictionary but larger, heavier, and with slightly stiffer pages. Each book contained an index of articles for current and past periodical articles on every subject.

That morning, before I began, I stood at the table quickly opening and closing the large books, knowing exactly what I was looking for. My stomach jumped when I located the first specific words I searched for alphabetically in the subject column on each page: "Fallopian tubes." It was there. I saw several abstracts—short summaries of articles—in the next column. The summaries also listed where, by whom, and when a specific article had been published.

Unstoppable

There were also "citations," which provided me with information needed to locate more articles on my subject.

I sat down at the table, holding the *Guide* open with my left hand and searching with my eyes as my right hand moved slowly down the small print. My eyes were immediately grabbed, as if by a magnet, to the words microsurgery, Fallopian tubes, infertility, ectopic pregnancy. I never once lost my focus. I had found the exact articles I needed. My pencil made a noise like the rubbing of fine sandpaper as I wrote the complete information I needed to give the librarian on small squares of paper. I had been sitting in the chair for two and a half hours without moving. Then I walked to the reference librarian's long counter, behind which were metal shelves with hundreds, maybe thousands, of boxes holding microfiche—holding the periodical articles I had just spent three hours perusing.

I turned back to the microfilm machine and looked at the boxes of as-yet-unread film. I saw my notebook filled with notes and realized that I was exhausted—still excited with all my discoveries related to Fallopian tubes and microsurgery, but exhausted.

I arrived back in the library basement first thing the next morning and walked straight to the counter. The librarian bent down, then handed me the stack of my unread boxes of microfilm, which she'd kept on hold for me overnight. I arranged the boxes on top of my green notebook and walked into the microfilm machine room again. I carried my schoolbooks stacked on my notebook just as I did as a schoolgirl.

"Let me load the first film for you to remind you exactly how to do it," the librarian said in a commanding whisper. She flipped the metal light switch on the machine and the screen illuminated in front of me. She loaded the first box of the *Journal of the American Medical Association* from January 1980 to May 1981. I flipped open my notebook and saw which months should have promising articles.

"The Use of Laser Surgery on Fallopian Tubes" was on the second reel of tape. I felt a cold breeze flush right across all of my skin. I shivered in the certainty that this technique was going to be it. Leaning forward and staring at the lighted screen, I read the short article describing a promising technique using minute laser beams to open occluded Fallopian tubes. Unlike the microsurgical technique using tiny tools, laser use resulted in far less tubal scarring during healing. This greatly reduced the risk of a fertilized egg getting caught on a bud of scar tissue in the tube and resulting in an ectopic pregnancy.

I sat back in my chair and considered this. So my embryo had become stuck on scar tissue. This clinical revelation made perfect sense to me. My local surgeon hadn't explained that to me, as he would not have been aware of the risks of the experimental microsurgery I'd had in Vancouver.

Now I raced back to the *Readers' Guide* and searched for more articles about laser surgery. The *New England Journal of Medicine* contained another similar article. I was as elated as if I had hit an ace on my tennis serve. I had a name: Dr. Michael Baggish was the surgeon using this technique at a hospital in Hartford, Connecticut. I felt an actual tingling in my chest as I wrote down his name. I cleaned up my microfilm machine area and returned the cardboard boxes to the reference librarian. As they tumbled onto the counter, she looked up at me.

"It looks like you found what you were looking for," she said. I slid the boxes across the counter. "You don't look as serious as you have the past two days. You have been looking as if your search was a life-or-death issue. It's nice to see you smile."

I drove straight home to the mountains up Ute Pass. Yellow-green buds were showing as I drove past steep hills covered with scrub oak. They hadn't dared open into full leaves yet, as frost and snow were still a possibility up in this altitude until late June. The miasma of color let me know that summer would be here soon.

On a page in my notebook, written in dark blue ink, I had a name. Dr. Michael Baggish.

Chapter 11

After finding Dr. Baggish's name in the basement library, I wrote him and asked if he'd be willing to talk to me about my situation and perhaps consider trying his new treatment—laser surgery—on me. I shared his reply one Sunday afternoon in mid-September as Peter watched a Broncos football game.

"So, I got a letter back finally from Dr. Baggish in Hartford, Connecticut," I told him. Peter seemed more intent on the game and eating chips than listening to me, which I was used to. "It's great news," I added. "He has me scheduled for surgery in November during my winter break. We can have Thanksgiving in Connecticut this year." Peter squinted and leaned in closer to the TV as though he couldn't see the screen or hear the sportscaster. I decided not to continue, as it was clear he was blocking me out.

"Now—what?" Peter said as a commercial came on. "What's this about Connecticut?" He sat back into the couch cushions and looked at me.

"Remember this summer when I told you about the article I found in the *New England Journal of Medicine* describing how a doctor in Connecticut was starting a trial using a laser to open Fallopian tubes?"

Peter didn't make a sound of recollection, so I leaned slightly forward and continued.

"His program just started this year. It's brand new. So I called his office. You took the message when his assistant called back, remember?"

Nothing.

"I had my medical records from Dr. Smith and Dr. Gomel sent to him."

Peter was still looking at me but hadn't spoken. I now felt like I was sucking all the air out of the room. I was in a one-sided conversation.

"He reviewed the records and accepted me into his laser trial. I just got the letter yesterday." I lowered my voice and stopped smiling. I was serious, very serious. "Peter, this is huge. It is a miracle that I even found out about this program and that we got in. We have to do it. I have to go. It is the only way I can get pregnant. I still have my right tube and I know he can open it."

"A laser, hmm," Peter thought aloud. "I didn't know they were being used for anything medical. One of the companies I trade is working on lasers, but for something called fiber optics. Maybe we should buy Teledyne options," he mused.

"Peter, 1 am scheduled for laser surgery on November 19th. It's in Hartford, Connecticut. Billy and Sue live there, so we can stay with them." Billy was my stepbrother.

"Are you sure you want to do this?" Peter asked after briefly sitting silent. "I don't like seeing my wife lying in a hospital bed looking gray. I really hate for you to go through this again."

"It is the only thing I want, Peter—a baby. Our baby. I have been searching for so long to find a new treatment for me and this is it. I really want to go. Please."

His concern had softened my tone and the delivery of my message. It was hard to know what he thought, as he was so reticent. His comment tugged at my heart. I didn't know until that minute that it hurt him to see me trying to recover.

Peter took a long time before answering. "Okay," he said. "Okay."

• • •

"Why didn't they close the airport? We are incredibly lucky our plane landed in this blizzard!" I said, squinting through the rental car window at the heavy snow falling all around us. It was snowing so hard that I could see rainbow colors, like the Northern Lights, flashing by in streaks and swirls.

"Lucky? Let's see if we make it to your family's house without careening off the road first. Then you can use the word lucky," Peter answered grimly. He was hunched forward in his seat, blinded by the snow and straining to see the road. The wipers scraped loudly as they raced at top speed over the iced windshield. Snow was clumping into enormous super flakes. It felt like we'd be buried under the weight of them if we didn't keep moving. Snow was piling on the hood of the car inches deep now and it looked like it would soon block our view completely. We would need to stop to brush it off, but I was afraid to stop.

The snow had so obliterated the afternoon sun it might as well have been the middle of the night. I was holding the letter—with directions—from my sister-in-law, Sue. The car heater roared loudly, blowing the paper covered with her curly handwriting. I reached down and opened the glove compartment for more light.

"Okay, look at Sue's directions and tell me where we get off this thing," said an annoyed, tense Peter, adding, "I hate New England snow." He had been raised in Boston.

"We are really close, I think. Let me look again. I just saw the sign for Simsbury," I said brightly, trying to lighten the mood.

We had arrived in this colossal nor'easter blizzard because I had found a new specialist and Peter had replied "okay" when I told him I had a surgery date. He did not share my excitement about having another surgery, yet he hadn't discouraged me from taking this step. He wanted a baby too. I was so relieved today when we landed at Bradley Airport, as I had been terrified for the past two months that Peter would say we couldn't afford this trip or say that he just didn't want to go. I had practically held my breath around him until I finally exhaled once we were sitting on the plane in Denver this morning.

I now gazed out at the snow-muffled rural Connecticut landscape. We hadn't passed many houses and I searched for street signs. Sue had told me that we would pass huge old tobacco barns where farmers used to dry tobacco. We came into a hilly area where a few signs appeared. I loved the New England names: Firetown Road, Old Farms Road, Salmon Brook Street, Hop Meadow.

"There it is. Meadow Crossing. Turn right. The house is the third on the right on Meadow Crossing. We made it!"

I had been to Billy and Sue's house in Simsbury before and knew my way around. They were in Mexico for the holiday. Sue had mailed a house key and the front door opened with one turn of the key and a solid push of my hip. Once inside the house, I took both of our heavy coats, opened the front hall closet door, and abruptly took a reflexive step backward. A tiny blue parka was hanging on the rod right in front of me. It looked like a doll's jacket next to the adult coats. It belonged to my nephew, who was a toddler. I couldn't look away. It was such a casual thing for a parent to do, leave the jacket in the closet and choose to dress the toddler in his warmer snowsuit. This was exactly the normal life I craved. The sight was both dear and heartbreaking. I knew I would remember that little jacket, a symbol of the nonchalant motions of parenting.

• • •

"Death-ray lasers are the only ones I have ever heard of." Peter smiled as he joked back to Dr. Baggish in our meeting at his office when the surgeon asked if we had heard of lasers before. "The kind aliens use to destroy humans and each other in science fiction."

"That is what everyone thinks when they hear the word laser," Dr. Baggish said in response. "Space alien lasers aren't what I use." He chuckled slightly.

He was an attractive man, probably in his forties. He had a tan face with strong, chiseled planes. I found myself thinking that his head would make a good bronze bust. We were in his office for our initial meeting that morning after an early drive back to Hartford over freshly plowed roads. Dr. Baggish had a serious demeanor. He didn't discuss our desire to have a baby. Instead, he elaborated on the experimental use of lasers. It was clear he was completely absorbed in their potential for remarkable medical use. He preferred to keep the discussion on a technological, and not a personal, level. On the wall I noticed framed certificates declaring that Dr. Michael S. Baggish had completed both an internship and residency at Johns Hopkins University School of Medicine. That gave me an increased confidence in his ability and training.

"A laser is a thin beam of extremely concentrated light. I am proving that a cleaner result will be the benefit of using the laser beam to excise scar tissue from Fallopian tubes. In microsurgery, as Mrs. Casey had in Vancouver, there is an incidence of resultant scarring. Unfortunately, we are seeing that the fertilized embryo can become caught on a bud of scar tissue and result in an ectopic pregnancy, as in your case back in April. My program is new, of course, but I am very pleased with the results I have seen so far."

Hours later, Peter and I had an early dinner at the Chart House. I had instructions not to eat or drink anything after 8 PM, as my surgery was scheduled for the next day. I had an apprehensive flutter in my stomach, so sitting at a twilight dinner with Peter was a perfect distraction. I had been so certain exactly one year ago this week—as I lay in that hospital in Vancouver—that having Dr. Gomel do microsurgery would end my desperation to redeem myself from using the IUD. After the first jolting pain of my tubal pregnancy, the reality hit me that I could no longer be certain. Even now. I had been innocent of tragedy before that day.

Peter's voice split my silent worries.

"I'll say this, Ellen, you have courage," he said, almost formally.

I looked across the table at him, hoping for more. But when he continued, he spoke of the book he was reading, *The Autobiography of Malcolm X*. Peter didn't even mention the topic of lasers, which I found an interesting omission. He didn't ask how I was feeling or if I was apprehensive about surgery. I knew that it made him uncomfortable to worry about me so it was easier to ignore the reason we were even in Hartford. The only comment he made about me was while discussing his book and how courage was a strong theme.

• • •

Two days later I lay quietly in a hospital bed under a pale cotton blanket. All I remembered of the surgery was feeling out of control, like I was trapped in a spider's web, and crying, "Help!" as the anesthesia started to overtake me. It felt like dying.

I looked around the room and noted yet again how colorless hospitals are. I thought of my acrylic paints at home and wondered how I could even mix them together to get the innocuous, drab color of the tray table next to me. The tray sitting on the table had a plate of food covered with a plastic lid that was another pale, sickly color.

The curtain surrounding my bed was suddenly whipped open. I flinched and gasped.

"Whoa. What's wrong? Why on earth did you jump like that?" Peter asked with a concerned expression. I didn't want to tell him.

"I thought it was going to be the doctor," I said.

"Why would you be scared when your doctor came in?" Peter asked.

"It hurts so much when they sit me up. The pain in my shoulder from the gas used during the laparoscopic procedure kills me. I don't want to say anything, but he must hear me gasp."

"Well, I don't like it that you flinched like that. Do you want me to talk to him?" Peter asked, frowning.

"No, no, no," I begged breathlessly. "Please don't. He doesn't mean to upset me. I know he is just doing his best to be sure he gets the results he wants from my surgery."

Just then the doctor entered my room, followed by two nurses, one of whom was holding a clipboard and pen. The doctor flipped through the sheets on the chart he was holding. I smiled brightly in greeting, and with my eyes dared Peter not to say a word. It was so important to me that I was likeable to the doctors and nurses. I know it was irrational, but I felt that when they liked me as a person, they would try even harder to help me have a baby.

So I said I wasn't in pain when I was and I said I was ready to get wheeled into yet another operating room when I wasn't. When the black terror of never having a child covered me like a shroud, I still smiled. I wanted every doctor and every nurse to know that I appreciated them so much. I always believe that if people know you like them and have confidence in their abilities, they will try harder to meet your expectations. It was a small way I could attempt to affect the outcome of what I so desperately wanted, knowing well that everything done medically was patently out of my control.

The doctor didn't make small talk but checked my sutures and said he wanted me to stay another day and night so he could be certain I did not develop an infection. When he said those specific words—"develop an infection"—I felt a sharp knife of concern. Now I would start worrying whether an infection was something that resulted after laser surgery, but I was terrified to ask right then. I did not want to appear to question his ability or technique, so I lay silent, pushing down my concern deep within. I was aware that my position of being in a bed put me at a disadvantage. It was a childlike, obedient posture.

Not a soul knew that I was in a constant state of fear that someone who had power over me, my husband or a doctor, would pronounce the word "No," and bring a huge iron door crashing down in my path, stopping me from continuing to try to have our baby.

"I will be back in tomorrow, and then we can discuss releasing you," the doctor said with such command that neither Peter nor I could think of a question to ask before he strode out of the room, followed closely by his note-taking nurse. I would have to spend at least another day and night in this hospital.

Dr. Michael Baggish and Laser Surgery

Dr. Michael Baggish, my surgeon at Hartford Hospital, was a pioneer in laser surgery, specifically in its use in gynecologic treatments. His successful experimentation resulted in many surgeons being trained to use the highly specialized laser to successfully open blocked Fallopian tubes.

The success of his work with lasers in the early 1980s is recognized nationally and internationally as medically groundbreaking. My laser surgery was performed in November 1980, making me one of his earliest patients.

Laser is an acronym for "light amplification by stimulated emission of radiation." The first working laser was created in 1960 by Theodore Maiman. The CO_2 laser produces a beam of infrared light and is used in place of a scalpel in surgery.

Dr. Baggish hypothesized that a laser, used on delicate Fallopian tubes, would result in less tissue damage than was caused by surgical instruments. The doctor mounted his carbon dioxide laser onto a laparoscope, which was inserted through my navel while I was under general anesthesia. Carbon dioxide was pumped into my abdomen to inflate it, giving the surgeon a less restricted view of my organs.

Viewing through the lighted laparoscope gave him the magnification necessary to do surgery on the tiny tubes with precise control. The scar tissue blocking my right Fallopian tube at its entrance to the uterus was vaporized by the incredibly accurate laser beam. A liquid was pushed into the tube to confirm that it was open.

Laser surgery is still done on Fallopian tubes today, but less often thanks to more recent advances in assisted reproductive technology, and in vitro fertilization—IVF.

Dr. Baggish continues to be a celebrated surgeon, teacher, and author of nearly 100 articles. His book, *Atlas of Pelvic Anatomy and Gynecologic Surgery,* coauthored with Mickey W. Karram, MD, is an invaluable reference for ob-gyn specialists, medical students, and surgeons.

Chapter 12

"No, no," I groaned, arms cradling my stomach. I was so sick. I knew I was going to vomit any second. When I tried to raise my head, I got so dizzy I thought I would faint. The room was spinning like I was on a horrible amusement park ride. My head was whirling out of control and my stomach was in agony. I could feel every hair on my body aching.

The ER nurse had given me a pink kidney-shaped throw-up tray and I was holding it on my lap as I doubled over. My right side felt so impossibly wrong and I could hardly bear the awful squeezing sensation. I didn't even pay attention as the nurse started an IV in my hand. I was so, so sick to my stomach.

Less than an hour earlier, my knees wobbled as I walked quickly into the pay phone booth outside the Safeway on West Colorado

Ave. I had just abandoned my cart full of groceries in the aisle when I felt the second pain. Dread made my skin ice cold. I felt like something inside of me was poking right through the soft skin of my abdomen. The laser surgery in Connecticut had been just six weeks ago, and I knew I wasn't pregnant.

I pulled the cloudy double doors shut behind me and picked up the tattered phone book that was attached to the counter by a thick cable. Someone had drawn cartoon faces on the cover with a ballpoint pen. I looked up Dr. Smith's office phone number. I slipped two dimes into the coin slot and heard them drop down with a clunk inside. I could see a distorted image of my face in the metal front of the pay phone. The phone was answered, "Colorado Springs Medical Center, Ob-Gyn Department. How can I help you?"

I described what I was feeling. The doctor came to the phone almost too quickly, I noticed. Doctors never come straight to the phone. Dr. Smith told me to meet him at the emergency room at St. Francis Hospital—about twelve minutes away.

"Do not drive yourself," he said. "Call Peter to come and get you or call an ambulance." I got into my own car anyway and drove to the hospital. I could feel the poke inside if I moved. I tried not to think, to keep my mind a disassociated, concentrated blank. I would not acknowledge consciously what I already knew. Something hideous was happening inside my body—again.

"Ellen, have you had any treatments other than the laser surgery since I have seen you?" Dr. Smith asked as he came rushing through the ER hallway toward me, his stiff medical coat flapping behind him. He frowned and looked concerned at my condition.

He held my medical file and lifted the typed pages that were clamped together at the top. It was a thick file, I noticed through my fog of suffering.

"No," I managed to respond, curled over so that my face was practically in my own lap.

"Start a saline drip right away," the doctor ordered. The nurse hung a thick plastic bag of clear liquid on a metal IV pole next to my bed. It clicked into place. I was throwing up without stopping. That made me feel worse, not better. Nothing was left in my stomach. I now had just the dry heaves and a horrible acidic rush tingled like pins in the glands under my jaw, like I had eaten a strong dill pickle.

"Ellen, I know you are feeling terrible," Dr. Smith said calmly, placing a reassuring hand on my shoulder. "But I have to examine you to see what is causing you to feel like this." The nurse tried to gently help me lie down as I gagged again. Dr. Smith pressed gently but firmly on my lower right abdomen directly above my ovary. "Is this where it hurts?" He didn't need to ask as I groaned, moved reactively from his touch, and threw up again.

"Can you describe the pain?" he asked while now pressing lower, below my hip bone. No sudden reaction from my body confirmed that this was not appendicitis. I knew what he was searching for. I registered all of his actions in my mind as I was silently begging for this agony to stop.

"My whole right side where the laser surgery was feels so sick. It isn't a sharp pain at all like the tubal pregnancy. This just feels like a sick aching, like I have been poisoned. There is something inside me that is poking out. It stabs me when I move."

"What is her temperature?" Dr. Smith asked the ER nurse. "Her other vitals?" I was burning up, but had thought until now that it was a reaction to my pain. A blood pressure cuff was curled around my arm and inflated.

"Ellen, you are not pregnant, are you?" he asked. I was positive I wasn't.

I heard him ask someone if my husband was in the waiting room. I hadn't called Peter when I first started feeling sick today at the grocery store. I was trying to handle this myself. I was afraid to upset him again.

"Did you get Mr. Casey's work number from Ellen when she registered? Good. Call him and have him come right down. He needs to get here now. Tell him that we will leave instructions at the emergency room desk where to meet me." I heard everyone, except for the nurse who was standing by my left hand with the IV drip, leave. They were talking in the hall.

I awoke in a different room, not knowing where I was or how I had gotten there. My head felt like it was on fire. Had I passed out? Slept? I felt panic but it was being held down by a blanket of heaviness that I couldn't shake away. I needed to think, but I couldn't get my brain to focus.

"Ellen, I am right here," Dr. Smith said as he picked up my limp hand and cupped it safely within both of his. He must have been standing next to me as my lids opened. He had seen the confused terror in my eyes. "We are getting ready to take you into surgery. There is a mass over your ovary and tube on the right side and it needs to be removed right now. Do you understand?"

"No," I whispered. I couldn't find my voice. "No. You have to save that tube. Please."

I had no strength and was fighting inside my burning brain to make sense of this. He could not remove my tube, and I had to make him know that. "Don't take the tube," I whispered as my head was being gently wrapped in a plastic cap.

"You just can't stay out of hospitals, can you?" Peter tried to make a joke as he walked in, looking so sad. He looked out of place in his black herringbone sports coat, white shirt, and tie. I knew he must have left his desk at Hutton in a rush to get to me when he got the nurse's phone call.

"Peter, help me. Tell the doctor he can't take my tube." I tried to push an urgent force into my words, but they came out so weak.

Peter looked paralyzed, and suddenly I was afraid. He cleared his throat. "I'll talk to him" was all he said, all he could say. I saw it in his eyes. He was helpless.

"Okay, Ellen, here we go," said a man in white who was next to me. He had just flipped up the metal railings on the sides of my bed and snapped them into place. Now he was somewhere behind me, and my bed began to move. A nurse laid her chart near my legs and helped him steer.

I looked for Peter; he was right beside me, walking slowly, looking at the floor. "Chin up," he said, stopping as the big metal doors swung open and I was swallowed into the operating room.

Chapter 13

I sat sideways on the living room couch with a yellow legal pad on my lap. The pad held pages of notes about medical treatments, which I had written in different colored inks over the past year and a half. Paper buckled up at the top in the shape of a wave from repeated flips through the sheets below. I moved to my left slightly to escape the discomfort of the enormous blue bandage covering the surgical wound I had received a week ago; it covered my entire abdomen. It rustled as I adjusted my position.

I stared out the picture windows at snow covering the mountains. It was February, still winter and already dark on our side of the mountains, as we faced north. I felt at home being in the shadows instead of in the bright sun, still gleaming across the way onto the south-facing slopes.

I turned to a clean page on my yellow pad, thinking of what I would put on a list of new ideas for how I would become a mother. A rapidly growing cyst had filled my left Fallopian tube. It had to be removed last week in emergency surgery along with my only remaining Fallopian tube. Dr. Smith explained to us that after he made the large incision and looked inside, he knew he needed to excise both tube and cyst, and do so immediately and carefully. There was no safe way to untangle the cyst from the tube. If the infected cyst had burst, dangerous septic poison would have spread into my entire peritoneal cavity, immediately putting my life in danger. Dr. Smith, always aware of preserving every facet of my fertility, did not remove my ovary, as probably any less-aware surgeon would have done. My fourth major surgery, and I was again back at home recovering with a painfully fresh, hip bone to hip bone, incision. At age thirty-two, I'd had surgery four times in the past fifteen months.

I was thinking about a phone call I had gotten five months earlier from my friend Cathy.

"Ellen," she had said, "I just saw a program today on surrogate mothers on *The Phil Donahue Show.*"

"What is that?" I asked, never having heard the term before. I played with the light blue phone cord as I listened.

"There is a program in Kentucky where women who want to help infertile couples have babies get paid to actually carry the baby, then give it to the couple. They use the couple's husband's sperm. After being pregnant with Andrew, I can't imagine being that altruistic," she laughed sarcastically, "but the surrogate mother Donahue had on today certainly was just that. She already had her own three children and didn't want any more. Her husband agreed she could do this for the couple who was on the show today with her. I think she was from Illinois. She got paid a lot, that's for sure—they wouldn't even say how much."

"Was she still pregnant or had she already had the baby?" I asked.

"Still pregnant. The couple was being really, really nice with her—fatuous, in fact. They said they sent her extra money for maternity clothes and sent gifts for her kids. I'll bet they are terrified she will change her mind and keep their baby. They never said that, though, on the show. They treated her like she was their best friend in the world. You should check into this."

Remembering back to that conversation, I now set aside my yellow pad and reached for the large envelope on the table next to the couch. Inside were printed transcripts from that *Donahue* show Cathy had told me about. The eponymous show, hosted by the energetic dynamo with thick white hair and dark glasses, was the most popular afternoon TV program for women. Phil would interview guests and then run offstage, holding his microphone and loose pages of notes, to take questions from the audience.

Over these past months my friends, who were at home while I was at work teaching, called often with reports of every lead they heard of for Peter and me to have a baby. My determination had rubbed off on them, and they'd joined me by looking for infertility treatment news both in print and on television. I had quite a collection of envelopes holding transcripts from this popular TV talk show, all wrapped together with a rubber band. After each friend's call about a pertinent program, I would type a letter to the Phil Donahue Transcripts address, shown on the screen at the end of each day's show, and request a specific transcript. With each letter I enclosed a check for $2.50 for printing and postage.

But this particular envelope held a very promising contact for us. His name was Dr. Richard M. Levin and he'd been on the *Donahue* show that Cathy had seen. He was the director of Surrogate Parenting Associates in Louisville, Kentucky.

After my first reading of the transcript, I had immediately called Dr. Levin's office. Even before my latest emergency surgery, Peter and I were already scheduled to travel to Louisville in May, as a brief but important stopover on our way to Ocho Rios, Jamaica, for a vacation. In Louisville we would attend a small meeting with the program's lawyer and doctor, leave a sample of Peter's sperm to be frozen, and also leave a large check, called a donation. I pictured a room with round stainless barrels full of long tubes, with dry ice billowing out frosty clouds when the lids were opened.

Knowing that I still had this plan B already in motion kept me from collapsing under the weight of again knowing I was physically unable to have a baby. I knew I could not get pregnant without at least one Fallopian tube, but I was not about to give up. I have always had a plan B for any problematic circumstance in my life, often plans C, D, and E as well. I was arranging those plans again right then. I would never, ever give up this quest for a baby.

I knew my tenacity ran in our family; I'd grown up hearing stories of how that came to be. I often thought about a story, famous in our family, about my Grandpa Weir—my dad's father. Daddy was a boy when it happened. Grandpa was a lawyer in downtown Cleveland, but the family of six children lived out in the country on the Weir farm in Hudson, Ohio. Grandpa had put himself through law school at night while supporting the family with his day job.

One evening, Grandpa had been out on the property riding his horse, Nero. When he didn't come home in time for dinner, the family began to worry. No one dared challenge Grandpa by going out to look for him. All six kids and their mother raced outside at the sound of the hooves of the tall black stallion as he finally cantered into the yard. Daddy's older brother, Don, reached up to hold the reins as Grandpa dismounted. His riding boots and jodhpurs were covered in light-colored mud. Nero had spray dashes of mud across his back, and his legs and stomach were thickly coated. He had white foam bubbles drying around his mouth.

No one spoke until Grandpa began telling them what had happened. Clarence, the groom, quietly took the horse's reins from Don and stood with the children, leaning in to listen. They had been deep in the woods when horse and rider became caught suddenly in a large pool of camouflaged quicksand. Shadows had covered the soaked sand in darkness, so they hadn't seen it looming right in front of them. Grandpa quickly realized they were both in mortal danger. No one escaped quicksand. Nero began to fight, even as his hooves were sinking deeper and deeper. Another horse would have given up and been pulled down, Grandpa told his rapt audience, but Nero had the heart of a thoroughbred. Grandpa used his voice and riding crop to encourage Nero. The horse kept fighting and fighting and Grandpa kept urging him to keep on, his knees squeezing into the English saddle leather. Grandpa said he had never imagined such strength or determination, and he felt as if horse and rider were one in this life-or-death fight. Nero never stopped for even one second, Grandpa said. He just kept fighting his way out of that quicksand. Courage, and a will to never stop trying, saved them both.

I knew I would never give up. If we adopted a baby, it would be mine. If we used a surrogate with Peter's sperm, that baby would be mine. I was positive that I would have a baby and it did not matter how we got it. I would not stop pursuing every possible avenue to realize my goal of being a mother until I held my child in my arms. I would never sink into the quicksand of surrendering to disappointment, grief, and loss.

Threaded through my multiple surgeries and doctor visits, I continued to pursue every possible option. The previous summer, a month and a half after my ectopic pregnancy, I visited a home for unwed mothers in Security, a small town south of Colorado Springs. My friend Laura had called and told me about it. Laura had lost a premature infant and later gave birth to two more children and adopted a daughter. She knew exactly how I felt losing my pregnancy and was doing what she could to help. This was a home facility, she told me, and was privately funded. Some of the mothers who stayed there gave their babies up for adoption, but many kept them. All of the mothers were young and had no family support. She felt I should visit and meet the women. Perhaps this could lead to an adoption for us, she hoped.

I called the manager of the home and asked what they needed. She suggested that I donate towels or sheets for twin beds. I parked in front of a nondescript house with white siding and checked again to be certain I had the correct address. I entered through the front door, my huge plastic bags overflowing with yellow bath towels, bathmats, hand towels, and washcloths. To my left was the living room where I waved a hello to six pregnant women sitting around talking and watching TV. I noticed that some were smoking, others were drinking Cokes. One had her hand in a large bag of potato chips. The house manager, a woman in her fifties, had let me in the door and took the bags from me with thanks. She introduced me to the women in the living room and told them I had brought new towels for them. She pulled out a bright yellow sample and waved it in their direction.

I entered the room knowing I had an important purpose, a clear goal. I hoped that one of these unwed mothers would decide to give her baby up for adoption. Give her baby to us. I wanted them to like me.

I sat to talk with the girls. I told them my story and explained how much we wanted a baby. I was uncomfortable watching their unhealthy prenatal behavior but tried not to let it show. A few seemed resentful, but not at me, I realized, after being shocked when an openly angry girl looked at me, swearing, "I hate that man. He is never going to see this child." Most were bashing men in general, the fathers of their babies in particular. I hadn't expected such a hostile environment. However, I knew that I was in a completely different situation than they. I was dying for a baby and they were alone, dealing with unplanned, unwanted pregnancies. Each one of them said she was going to keep her baby.

I left my name and phone number with the manager when I left after an uncomfortable twenty minutes, but did not expect, nor did I receive in the year that followed, a call saying one of the residents wanted to have her baby adopted.

Another option I'd tried was adoption through Lutheran Social Services. Friends had heard of couples who were able to adopt through them, but I knew of no one who had actually gotten a baby. I was apprehensive that I would have to sell the idea of adoption to Peter. I was so relieved when he agreed with me when I said firmly that any baby who came into our home would be ours.

I got a stomachache every time I presented a new plan to Peter. I just couldn't gauge how he would react. I was constantly thinking of ways to have a baby. Anxiety and preoccupation with research had become overwhelmingly predominant in my inner life. Having a baby was all I thought about. I couldn't help but worry that one day Peter might balk. I did not discuss what I was working on until I had already contacted the medical programs and doctors. I still felt the whole thing was my fault, so this had to be my search. I was totally committed. There was no reason to burden him constantly with my anguished drive for a baby. I just prayed that he would continue to support me.

"Sure," he said about the Lutheran agency. "You take care of working out the details and just tell me when and where I am supposed to show up." Yet again I was thankful Peter was so relaxed and easygoing. It did cross my mind that he was disinterested in this quest of mine. He was so quiet. Still, I felt reasonably certain that he would continue to go along with me. He was devoted to me and knew how much I wanted a baby. Plus, adopting through a local agency meant no travel and he wouldn't have to be away from studying the stock market the way he did. Each night at home he charted the trends, the highs and lows of certain stocks, and every day he made trades and recommendations from his office at E. F.

Hutton. I relaxed when I learned that the upcoming group meeting with Lutheran Social Services would be in the evening and wouldn't require him to leave work to attend with me.

So, on August 28, 1980, Peter and I walked into a downtown church meeting room where about twenty anxious, hopeful couples were already sitting in metal folding chairs. The atmosphere was tense, like a room full of adults who were waiting for college acceptance letters at the same time. A few steps inside the door was a woman who identified herself as director of the adoption program, standing behind a long table. She checked our names off her list of attendees and handed us a stack of papers.

I smiled warmly at her, wanting her to like us best. I felt like she held such power over us in our quest to adopt. Some of the papers had information and contact numbers. Some had so much information that I would have to read them later. Peter and I sat down, speaking quietly as the other couples were, and filled out information forms on clipboards. The room was quiet as we all waited for the speaker to begin.

I studied the other prospective parents, feeling suddenly competitive with them. I wondered if they wanted a baby as much as I did. I was confident knowing I certainly must have more irons in the fire, more plan Bs, than the others did. Still, I worried that one of these couples might get "our" baby.

The meeting lasted just over an hour. The female speaker, in direct contrast to the tense anxiety of her audience, dispassionately described the program, requirements, and current time frames. Audience members raised their hands, anxious to voice their intensely delivered questions, which were startling in contrast to the speaker's reserve. It reminded me of the hands that were raised so high in the air at Laurel as we girls were intent on giving the correct answer or posing the strongest argument in class. One man asked if twins were ever available. She answered that birth mothers usually decided to keep twins, as a multiple birth was so unique. Another asked how often parents changed their minds after the baby was born.

I hung my head in dejected disappointment as we left. I was scuffing my feet on the loose gravel. We walked through the church parking lot silently. Peter's arm was tight around my shoulder, although he didn't say anything. We had learned that the wait to adopt an infant was four years through the Lutheran program. We were already thirty-one, and in four years would be thirty-five— over their age limit to adopt.

• • •

It was an early evening in late October and the sky was threatening snow. The phone rang. I ran across the living room to answer it and heard the voice of my cousin. She was calling from her home in Los Angeles. "Ellen," she said, "we have friends whom we've known since we were all at UCLA Film School. The husband is in film and his wife is a film editor. We saw them this weekend and got to meet their adorable baby girl. They adopted her when she was just a few days old through a private attorney in San Francisco."

I sat down in the chair next to the phone to listen, crossing my legs and kicking one foot nervously. "I told Missy, the wife, about everything you have gone through. She said she had such a similar story and that they were so thrilled with this precious little daughter. Missy said it would be best for you to call her directly and she would tell you about their adoption process and give you all the details to contact their lawyer."

Peter came home and sat on the couch to watch *Monday Night Football*. We had finished our tacos and I went upstairs to our loft bedroom, holding the phone number for my cousin's friends. I sat on the bed next to the phone and called. The husband answered the phone on the third ring. Even though I knew who he was, a famous writer and director, I just calmly introduced myself and explained why I was calling. I waited for his wife to come to the phone, as he said with some humor in his voice, "Missy knows all of the details, and you would be much better off talking to her." He laid the receiver down and I heard him call for her. I waited.

When Missy picked up, she already knew who I was and put me immediately at ease. The lawyer they had used to facilitate their adoption was not an adoption attorney, but a personal friend, she said. She gave me his name and contact information. She hoped that he could help us. When I walked downstairs after hanging up the phone and told Peter the name of the movie director to whom I had just spoken, he didn't believe me. When I explained the connection to my cousin, he just laughed, shook his head, and commented appreciatively, "Of course you just called him from our bedroom. Only you, Ellen, only you. You amaze me."

That night I again sat at the dining room table typing on my humming electric typewriter. So excited with this lead, I got more and more frustrated as I kept having to pull the sheet of paper out of the rubber rollers and put in a fresh piece. I was typing so fast that my mistakes were many. I did not want to use typing correction strips on this letter, as I wanted it to look perfect. I knew I needed to slow down. I wrote a formal letter to the lawyer. Ten days later I received a cool response giving me a price for his services that was more than a year's college tuition. I was stunned. He also said that babies were very difficult to find for a clean legal adoption. He would be in touch when and if the situation of an available baby arose and thanked me for contacting his office.

I knew that if he ever called with an adoptive baby for us, I would manage somehow to find the funds to pay him. Though this option didn't sound to me as if it was worth spending more time pursuing, I wrote back and assured him that we most certainly wanted to be on his adoption list. He never got back in touch with us, although I wrote a follow-up letter a month later.

• • •

Back in 1980, while still reeling emotionally from my ectopic pregnancy, I had pulled out the baby-blue electric typewriter my father had given me in high school, plugged it in, and began to type. The machine hummed loudly as the keys clicked. I wrote a formal query to the Drs. Jones at Eastern Virginia Medical School. I had read in the newspaper that Howard and Georgeanna Jones had been approved to open the very first in vitro fertilization clinic in the United States in the fall of 1979. I had researched their clinic on microfiche in the library basement and located an address.

As I typed, I carefully and concisely explained my current medical situation following the microsurgery in Vancouver. I asked that

Peter and I be put into immediate consideration for a place in their new program. I was excited to know that I had a plan B, thanks to this new technology.

I received a return letter that was dated June 16, 1980. I cringed when I saw that the salutation read "Dear Patient." This was not a personal missive to me but a form letter. My stomach lurched when I read "At this time, there are over 6,000 names on our list." I couldn't believe that many couples had gotten in touch with the clinic in the three brief months that the IVF program had been open. "Your letter will be placed on file and please be assured that we will be in touch with you at the earliest possible time. Our waiting list is currently five years, or more, long."

In five years, I would be thirty-six years old and would have aged out of their in vitro program. The requirements stated in this letter were that the mother had to be thirty-four years or under. My hopes sank, but only briefly. I was certain that if one program had gotten government approval to open, others would follow. A year and a half after their program was approved, on December 28, 1981, baby Elizabeth Jordan Carr was born through the Joneses' in vitro program. The United States had its first test-tube baby.

I knew then, I was absolutely positive, that I, too, would have a baby.

Chapter 14

I stepped into the teachers' lounge. A pink slip of paper caught my eye, sticking partially out of my faculty mailbox in the school office. I recognized that it was a phone message torn off the notepad our secretary used. I slipped it out of the wooden cubby and read the words she had written. She had filled in the caller line with the name "Alice at Dr. John Smith's office" followed by the phone number and message "Call today." I didn't know what this was about, other than that Dr. Smith was my gynecologist and surgeon for both emergency surgeries, so I went straight to the phone booth and dialed the number.

A receptionist who answered was expecting my call. She asked what day I might be able to come into the office to meet with Dr. Smith this week. I scheduled for that same afternoon, intrigued by this unexpected invitation. It was like hearing the scratch of a match being struck in the darkness and suddenly seeing a minute flame illuminate the blackness. Dr. Smith wanted to talk to me.

Hours later, I sat in a chair in the waiting room noting darkly that every single woman in the room was pregnant. *No*, I reminded myself, *every single* other *woman in the waiting room is pregnant. I am not.* It must have been a day for prenatal exams. Each time I heard the elevator bell ding loudly, announcing doors opening onto this, the OB floor, I tried not to look up to see who would step out. I knew it would be another woman my age or younger in her flowy maternity top billowing softly over maternity pants. The polyester pants were so ugly. And, I would have given anything to be wearing a pair myself.

"Hello. I see you are here for your five-month, or eight-month, or any-other-month gestational visit," I heard the receptionist say brightly as a parade of patients checked in at the desk. I felt lonely and sad in my belted jeans and tan Frye boots. I was tired, worn out, and it washed over me that I might cry. I did not belong in this room of mothers.

I hoped no one would notice me. I wanted to slide down in my seat so that I could disappear. Head down, I reached to the side table next to me where my sole choice of magazines was past and current issues of *Parents* magazine. I was assaulted by large-print cover articles: "A New Baby! How Parenting Improves Your Marriage," and "S*P*A*C*I*N*G* Children," casual references to the ease of getting pregnant. I sobbed inside. My throat clamped shut like I couldn't swallow. I had to fight the urge to dash to the elevators or run to the door to the stairs; I just wanted to escape to someplace where I could cry forever.

"Ellen Casey?" called a uniformed woman holding a clipboard, looking into the sea of mothers-to-be in the waiting room. I was so relieved to slip, eyes downward, over to her side of the counter and be ushered away into an exam room. "How are you today?"

"Fine," I answered, not meaning it at all. Inside I heard the echo of my genuine, yet unspoken words, "Devastated and broken, but trying to look positive to you so you won't give up on me."

I was constantly, consciously so terrified that if I ever gave my doctors or my husband any idea of how shattered and desperate I was inside, they could and would put a stop to my determined quest to have a baby. It was a constant, knee-shaking reality to know that other people—all men, in fact—had such staggering power over my life. I was well aware that they did, however, and I knew I would speak and present myself in any way necessary to keep them on my side. So, I morphed into my practiced actress mode. Mother often referred to me as "Pollyanna," but she didn't know how hard I worked to sustain the act. She didn't know that being called "Pollyanna" stung.

"I am just fine, how are you?" I added with a smile as we entered the small examination room. These rooms all looked the same to me at this point. I had seen far too many over the past four years. There was always the hard plastic bed covered with wide white paper on a roll behind it that was pulled off and changed between patients. Cold metal stirrups tucked down at the far end of the bed made me think of a tool of torture in the Tower of London. The room was so impersonal that I never once wondered about the woman who had been in it before me, nor the one who would enter when I left. Were they happy, worried, loved? The room was blank and undecorated. I quickly looked away from a model of a cross-section fetus, head down, just above the birth canal, sitting on the counter next to the sink.

I didn't know why I was here for this appointment and hadn't asked. I assumed that the doctor just wanted to confirm that the wound from my latest emergency surgery, following the laser in Connecticut, was continuing to heal nicely. The actress in me was also very smooth at brightly acknowledging that term, "healing nicely," when inside I only remembered the sad cause of every recently stitched emergency incision that seemed to be doing so well.

I was so tired of carefully arranging my calm façade when inside I felt ransacked.

There was a polite knock as the door swung open and Dr. John Smith entered. I admired and respected him. He had been the emergency surgeon for both of my crisis surgeries. I knew that he focused on doing the least internal damage possible even as he operated to save my life. He was acutely aware that every surgery results in scarring and that intrauterine scars were the roadblock to fertility in women. He supported me completely in my quest for the medical treatment that would one day result in me finally becoming pregnant. He always discussed with me the newest success in infertility treatment findings released at the American Fertility Society (known today as the American Society for Reproductive Medicine) conferences he attended.

I appreciated that he talked to me as an equal. He often photocopied articles for me from his medical periodicals. He was in contact with the specialists I had seen and had complete copies of all of their surgical notes. And, of critical importance to me, he was smart. He listened to me seriously. I knew that he respected me for researching infertility medicine so diligently and for managing to arrange to have surgery performed by both the microsurgery pioneer, Dr. Gomel in Vancouver, and laser pioneer, Dr. Baggish in Hartford. I think he was both bemused and impressed when I told him that I had taken Peter to Surrogate Parenting Associates in Louisville.

Dr. Smith smiled and shook my hand. He was holding my medical file, which was now about four inches thick with pages and pages of charts, records, and notes on different colors of paper. He sat in the chair at his desk, crossed his right leg over his left knee, and with the warmest smile I had ever seen, he said, "Guess what?"

"What?" I leaned forward slightly and smiled back, noticing excitement emanating from his light blue eyes that were looking straight into mine.

"The University of Texas Health Science Center in Houston has just been approved this week to begin operation of an experimental in vitro fertilization program. I called their office and have all of the required application information for you." He reached back for a large manila envelope that he had dropped lightly on his desk just after we shook hands. I saw that it was hand-addressed.

"Inside this are all of your medical records the program requested when I spoke with them."

I was stunned and felt my face flush. He flapped the envelope for me to take it from his hands. I involuntarily held my breath. He was handing me hope in a mailing envelope. He had addressed it himself and filled it with my medical records.

Dr. Smith had just saved my life today. I was certain of it.

This individual doctor's strength of character shown in such active concern for one small patient was my pathway to acceptance into the newest IVF program in the United States. I would be accepted. I knew it. I knew I would have a baby. My mind was racing.

"Breathe!" he said, noting that I hadn't moved at all since his remarkable announcement. "You must show proof that you are a legally married couple before they will even consider you, so I want you to get a photocopy of your marriage license. Write an application letter to Dr. Martin Quigley at the address on this envelope and follow the rest of the instructions I have written inside for you. Get it in the mail today. I think you have a very good chance of being accepted into the program, as no one even knows that it exists yet."

Chapter 15

"Please, God, please." I briefly closed my eyes as I whispered the words. "Let me have a test-tube baby, and I promise you I will tell everyone about it. I promise I will let every other infertile couple, people just like Peter and me, know that there is a new chance for them to have a baby. I will talk to the press so that everyone can learn about in vitro fertilization. I know that there is a reason we have this chance to go to Houston to see if I qualify for surgery. Please, God, let me be able to get into this program. Please, God, let us have our baby at last. Please."

I leaned against the brick school wall that had been absorbing the strong Colorado sunshine all day. In response to the rush of surprising warmth on my back, I felt a little shiver run across my skin and down my spine. My kindergarteners were playing in front of me in our fenced playground just steps outside of the classroom door. "Please, God, I have loved so many little children as a teacher. I have genuinely loved the little children in my classes for eleven years," I prayed. "They know I love them. You know I love them. Please, please, isn't it time I can love a child of my own?"

I wished out loud for a child on the evening star every night. "Star light, star bright, first star I see tonight, I wish I may, I wish I might, have the wish I wish tonight." I knew the first star we saw each night just over the 14,000-foot Pikes Peak, the star I wished on religiously, was actually the planet Venus. I kneeled at Grace Episcopal Church on Sundays and prayed for a baby. Was I praying wrong? In my prayer today I made a new plea, as I had made so many different promises before. The muscles around my ribs tightened like a corset as I tried to find the perfect words that God wanted to hear.

A month later my forehead rested against the cold oval window of the plane as I remembered my playground prayers. It was now July 11, 1982, and Peter sat next to me as the plane slowly descended over Texas. I shivered again, but not from the cold of the window glass; I was excited and terrified in equal measure. We were flying into Houston for our appointment to meet Dr. Quigley tomorrow morning. This was our first step to get into his test-tube baby program.

"You are clenching your thumbs inside your fists again," Peter commented from my left. "Worried?" he asked.

"No, I'm excited. I still can't believe we are going to land in Houston any minute," I answered. Peter raised his dark eyebrows in a sign of questioning my words as I looked over at him. "Well, okay," I conceded, "of course I'm nervous, but I am not worried."

After a pause, I shook my head in a "no" movement acknowledging the gravity of this visit. "This is just so important. But it is going to work, I know it." I felt my fingers wrap around my thumbs even more tightly. I looked out the window again. "I didn't know Houston had this many lakes. You should see all the docks and boats out there." I changed the subject and Peter was quiet in his seat next to me.

While I sat on the end of the unmade bed and waited for Peter to finish reading so we could leave for our doctor's appointment, I tried to make sense of what happened to me last night and again this morning in our Houston hotel. In my life, I have never had trouble sleeping. I sleep solidly, never waking in the night, just as Daddy always had. My insomniac mother used to joke wryly, "If your father was going to be executed at dawn, he'd still get a good night's sleep." I had inherited his sleep gene, she said. But, last night in the hotel I had hardly been able to get to sleep. I have always been focused, driven, goal oriented, but never anxious. I had given myself the hiccups after dinner in the hotel restaurant, which Peter found hilarious. Being this anxious to an extreme was a new feeling for me. I didn't like how hard my heart was beating. I felt a strange pressure on my chest, like I couldn't catch my breath. My mind was jumping from thought to thought wildly, like a bird trapped inside a building. Finally, I got out of bed, walked around the room in the dark, tried deep breathing alone in the bathroom, and finally fell asleep in bed.

This morning I awoke early, acutely aware that I couldn't move. I was completely paralyzed. I couldn't open my eyes. I couldn't move my arms or legs. "I am in a coma," I thought in terror. My brain was totally awake and was racing through every possibility for this total paralysis. "Okay—one, two, three," I thought, "open." But my eyes did not respond. I could even sense Peter's warmth in bed next to me, but I couldn't move any of my muscles. I couldn't even open my eyes. "I am in a coma," I thought again. I just had to lie there. I tried futilely to scream. But I could not move. I could not scream. My brain was completely aware of where I was, and it was in a full-blown state of panic. The next thing I knew I bolted up into a sitting position, gasping loudly for air like a person rising to the surface after nearly drowning.

"Whoa, what was that?" Peter asked from his pillow facing away from me.

"I couldn't move. I was just paralyzed. I mean it. Paralyzed. It was the worst thing," I whispered. I was inhaling long deep breaths to prove to myself that I was still alive.

"Hmmm," Peter turned over onto his back and looked up at me with a puzzled expression on his sleepy face. I realized that I had to calm down right away so he didn't think I was crazy, so he wouldn't reconsider why we had come to Houston.

"It must have just been a dream," I muttered dismissively and shook my head to get rid of the horrifying memory. I knew that it had been no dream. What had just happened was real. And it was terrifying.

"Hmmm." Peter looked away from me and sat up with his long legs flipped over the side of the bed. He briefly rubbed his forehead. "And you say you aren't worried? You are giving yourself nightmares."

• • •

I had imagined this place so many times and suddenly, strangely, there we were. I stood motionless, arms dragged down as if weighted, head tilted upward, staring at numbers stenciled in heavy black above the large glass doors. 6431 Fannin. I had seen that address on envelopes, large and small, since the spring day when Dr. Smith had handed me my medical records inside the manila mailing folder. A tingle tickled my skin and I shuddered in excitement. This address had been the only place I wanted to be for months. I felt like a six-year-old seeing the sparkling entrance to Disneyland from across the parking lot. My wish had come true and my cheeks ached from smiling so hard. We were there. *Here.* I heard Peter's voice behind me thanking the taxi driver and then the sound of the yellow cab slowly pulling away from the curb.

"Well, shall we go in or should we just stand here?" Peter joked, coming up behind me. I turned to face him. "Look at that smile." He placed his hand on the small of my back and guided me toward the doors. I was clutching a folded piece of paper on which I had quickly jotted the instructions in blue ballpoint ink, given to me over the phone at home in Colorado.

They read: "Under tunnel, med. school, yellow elev., 3d, turn lf. twice (chapel out window), go to orange in front."

These abbreviations had made sense when I wrote them, and now I wasn't certain what some of them even meant. I felt suddenly unsure of myself. "Do you know where we are going?" asked Peter.

"I do," I answered, holding up the paper. I would get us to the doctor's office.

Even though I said "third floor" out loud after looking somberly at the paper in my hand, we still both looked at a black board with names and floors and office numbers in white lettering just to the left of the silver elevators, for confirmation. Then, without speaking to each other, we looked up at the numbers above the elevator doors, watching as they lighted up to show the descending elevator's progress.

"Here we go," Peter, hand on my back again, said after all the people had walked off and into the lobby. I heard a woman laugh as she passed me. I was holding my breath again as the doors closed behind us and the elevator started to move, pressing me into the floor ever so slightly.

"Turn left twice," I read, consulting my paper. I took a deep breath, the kind you hold for two long counts in the very bottom of your lungs, then blew the air out shakily. After the second left turn, I spotted the chapel across the street in the hospital building. I remembered now why that was in my directions as a landmark. We were going the right way. Then the orange counter with "Medical School Department of Obstetrics, Gynecology and Reproductive Sciences" appeared right in front of us. I stepped confidently in front of Peter and walked right up to the receptionist. I was holding an official letter inside an envelope with my appointment date and time inside. I worked to push down the voice of fear that tried to fill my ears. This envelope gave me concrete affirmation that we were really expected today, and I laid it on the counter. I was so afraid I would be told to go home. I was terrified we wouldn't get into the program. So I stood up tall and confidently said, "Ellen and Peter Casey to see Dr. Quigley."

"Congratulations," the pretty blond woman surprised me by answering. She smiled at both of us. I turned to look at Peter and we both burst into huge grins. I even shrugged in surprised elation at her word. "Congratulations."

"That was cool," I said quietly as we sat down in the waiting room, even though we were the only people there. A door opened to our left and a young woman said, "Mr. and Mrs. Casey, please come right in. Dr. Quigley is ready to meet you in his office." Peter reached down and took my hand. He never held hands with me, as he said it made him feel like he was "walking a dog." I sensed my face brighten as I smiled through closed lips and held on tightly with a quick squeeze.

Dr. Quigley's door was open. He stood up as we entered and walked around to the front of his desk to shake hands with each of us. *He is darling*, I thought. He exuded warmth, not formality, yet carried himself assuredly. He was tall and had happy, brown eyes twinkling over pink cheeks. I knew absolutely nothing about this doctor before walking through his door. There was nowhere I could research him, no biography in the library. I had to put all of my trust, and my very last hope to have a baby, in him. His demeanor made that remarkably easy. The fact that he was the head of this nascent test-tube baby program at the University of Texas gave me all the belief in his medical acumen I needed.

Dr. Quigley returned to his desk. Peter and I sat in chairs facing him.

"Rumor has it that you want to get pregnant," he said with a smile.

I laughed aloud and responded, "Oh, what gave you that idea?" glancing pointedly across the desk at the thick patient file lying under his palm. I knew it held all the records from my past three years of unsuccessful attempts at reversing my infertility caused by blocked Fallopian tubes.

I registered that both the receptionist's and Dr. Quigley's very first words to us had the effect of putting us into an immediate and relaxed ease. I was even more positive about this program. We were clearly being treated differently, not as "just patients." I sensed that we were special and as if we were all in this together. Then the doctor introduced us to two other people who were already inconspicuously inside the room when we entered. One was a young male intern and the other a female ob-gyn resident. He explained that they would observe the interview. I wondered if they were studying the doctor-patient personal interaction as much as listening to the medical information that would be discussed.

Dr. Quigley explained to us that he would perform a screening laparoscopy tomorrow to determine if there was sufficient area of my ovaries free from scar tissue to enable removal of eggs to be fertilized outside of my body. I would be put under general anesthesia. He would then view my ovaries through a laparoscope inserted through my navel. He went on to explain the actual process of in vitro fertilization, but my brain had stopped at tomorrow's procedure. I knew the laparoscopy was really all that mattered. The importance of tomorrow caused everything else in my brain to completely black out.

Tomorrow would be the day I would know if I could ever have my own baby. My ears filled with white noise and I could think of nothing but tomorrow.

Chapter 16

In a freezing rush, goose bumps covered my arms. It felt like icy drizzle was slowly pouring down my back. I thought of wet little boys huddling by the pool, shivering, their lips pale blue. I had just changed into a hospital gown for surgery. I crossed my arms across my chest and scrunched closer into myself.

My yellow summer sundress, worn for the Houston heat, and the rest of my clothes were inside of a gray hospital locker in the pre-op changing room. As I was led by a woman into the space, I recognized the same brand of lockers from the gym at home where Peter and I worked out most afternoons. I already knew how to use the combination lock on the door, although the friendly volunteer carefully helped me anyway. I was struck by how this was not at all like casually leaving my clothes in the locker at Nautilus in Colorado Springs. Although the two lockers were identical, the process the same, this time before I pressed the door closed I stared thoughtfully at my folded clothes. I consciously wondered what I would know when I saw that yellow dress again.

Peter and I were sitting together in the waiting room at the Day Surgery Unit. I shivered again. I was feeling more nervous than I ever had before one of my scheduled surgeries, my thumbs tightly squeezed inside my fingers. This time was very different. In the waiting rooms before my microsurgery and laser surgery, I had a strong hope that each, performed by a gifted surgeon, would be a success. Today, success would be determined solely by the amount of scar tissue on my ovaries—and that was that. It would be decided by my body, not by the doctor's skill. By the time we left the hospital this afternoon, I would know if I could ever have a baby. In vitro fertilization was my last chance.

"Why am I doing this again?" The thought appeared a second and then a third time. I worked hard to force it out of my consciousness, but it kept popping back up like some bouncing creature in a crazy cartoon.

Peter had looked at my worried face earlier that morning as we rode through Houston in the taxi. He said that I didn't have to have this laparoscopy today if I didn't want to. "I didn't marry you for your childbearing capability," he said in a joking but also serious tone. I wondered if he would be relieved if I said, "Forget it, then. Turn the cab around!" But I put that out of my mind and stared out the windshield.

A nondescript orderly dressed in green wheeled a cart into the room where Peter and I sat. "Here we go, Mrs. Casey," he said in an upbeat manner. I turned to hug Peter before being helped up onto the gurney. My throat closed suddenly and I could feel my eyes stinging. I just couldn't bear to leave Peter this time and had to force myself to let go of his strong hug. All I could do to hold down the terror that was quickly overtaking my body was to hold my breath, again.

"Good luck" was really all he could say. This was the fifth time he had said good-bye to me as I was wheeled away to surgery.

The orderly checked my hospital wristband and compared it to his clipboard notes. "Yup," he said, "it's you!" I couldn't respond with a smile. I could feel all of my nerve and bravery melting away like snow in the sun. I stared up at row after row of lights on the ceiling as he pushed me through the halls. He stopped in an open room where I saw four pre-op patients hooked up to IVs. My bed was parked at the outer edge of the group. I looked away from the others.

A nurse wheeled a small metal cart across the floor and pushed it to a stop next to me. She pulled a rolling stool over in a practiced, quick spin and stopped it with a firm slap of her hand on the vinyl seat. A moment earlier she had guided a rattling IV pole from the same direction and placed it behind my left ear. I knew it was there but couldn't see it in my peripheral vision. It had sounded like the dreaded broken grocery cart at the store whose wheels didn't all move in the same direction. I noticed that she was serious about her work, frowning as she lifted clear plastic tubing in coils from her cart, looking for something underneath. She didn't speak and seemed not particularly interested in me. As she ripped open a small paper wrapper that was covering a needle, I started to cry silently inside. I quickly clenched my stomach muscles to try and stop my tears and held my breath aggressively. I pressed my breath as hard as I could deep into my diaphragm. In response to my movement, the nurse looked over at me.

"Are you scared?" she accused, in a flat voice. She sat still, watching as I wiped away rolling tears with the back of my hand. I caught my breath again and tried to hold it in to force my tears back inside. I nodded in response to her question but could not manage words to answer.

She didn't say anything but turned back to my left arm that she had just pulled straight and long beside me. She began sharply tapping the veins on top of my hand. She tapped again and a third time before stabbing a needle that looked like a tiny pin into the top of my hand. It hurt, but I didn't pull away. After a moment, she removed it and looked at my face with a scowl.

"Your veins are collapsing because you are so upset," she reprimanded. "I have seen surgery canceled because a patient was too nervous," she warned brusquely.

"You don't understand," I wanted to whisper. "This is so, so important." I wanted to tell her that I was brave. I wanted her to know I was afraid of the outcome, but not of the surgery itself. She had spoken to me like I was a wimp. I saw her turn her back to me and stalk away. I couldn't believe that at this late time in my quest to have a baby I was coming unglued at the seams. I felt like I was dissolving. I wanted to rush into a bathroom and sob violently alone, then pull myself together and return to the bed composed again. I had to have this surgery today. I couldn't be so upset that she would cancel it. Now I had a new terror convulsing my stomach. Did she have the power to cancel my surgery? I knew I was breathing too fast, like I was running in fear for my life.

The nurse returned with a folding screen covered in pleated cream sheeting and arranged it around me without speaking. Now I was alone and couldn't see anyone else. I pulled every cell of my body together and willed myself to relax, eyes closed. "I will do this," I knew, and thought of getting out of quicksand. "I can do this," I told myself calmly, eyes still closed and concentrated on quieting my breathing. I slowly counted as I breathed in through my nose, out through my mouth.

The screen moved aside slightly and in walked Dr. Quigley. He was dressed in his operating scrubs, complete with green booties covering his shoes.

"I understand you are climbing the walls out here," he said so kindly my heart ached. I responded immediately to his avuncular demeanor. He placed a warm hand on my shoulder while he spoke to me. I felt myself relaxing under his touch and slipping into the calm of his soothing voice. It was the voice of a friend. I knew if I attempted to explain to him why I was so upset, so terrified that this surgery today could be the end of my road, I would cry again. Yet, it seemed my doctor already knew exactly what I was both thinking and feeling.

Each woman seeking acceptance into the in vitro program needed to undergo this critically important laparoscopy. I was guessing I was not the first to feel this wave of anxiety shatter my composure. He wisely maneuvered the subject away from me and began to describe the surgery he had just completed. It was a tubal ligation, which I found ironic. I asked if he had children and he mentioned small boys. By the time the nurse reentered my screened-in area, she was easily able to slip the needle into my hand and attach it to the IV cable.

"See you in a minute," Dr. Quigley said, squeezing my shoulder gently. As he walked around the screen to exit, I heard him direct the nurse to start a Valium drip. I managed to chuckle as I pictured her smug agreement to that order. I closed my eyes and relaxed. "I can do this."

I tried not to think as I was wheeled into the operating room. "This is not real," I pretended. The anesthesiologist introduced himself. I asked if he would please alert me before he put me under. I have had nightmares of the room swirling around and around like a spinning colored toy, blocking out my mind, blocking out me, since having surgery for my broken wrist at age ten. I have been afraid of anesthesia and the resulting total loss of control ever since. Two gowned nurses spoke to me as they stood on either side of the cart. Each patted me gently.

Just then, a memory of the previous weekend appeared in my mind. Peter and I had hiked up the Ute Creek Trail on a clear blue Colorado day. We had stopped for a snack and drink of water when suddenly a huge insect buzzed loudly around my head and attacked my hair. I was startled and flailed my arms over my head, ducking away from the sound. I heard the loud buzz stop in a small oak right next to me. I looked up and there was a tiny hummingbird sitting motionless on a branch. What I had perceived as so scary and dangerous was actually an exquisite, delicate creature, kaleidoscope colors glistening in the sun. We looked right at each other. I heard the message of this encounter as if it had been spoken to me over a megaphone. This was my last image as the doctor said, "Okay, Ellen, you are going to go to sleep now."

Peter was waiting in the recovery room for me. After what seemed like a short time to regain alertness and the ability to think, I begged to know what the doctor had found. My mind was still fuzzy around the edges, but I knew I had to hear the results. Peter and the recovery nurse looked at each other. The nurse picked up my chart, trying to be helpful. She read aloud from the surgical notes, "80 percent of left ovary . . . adhesions . . . 60 percent of right." I was devastated and felt myself sinking. It was over. I had lost.

Dr. Quigley must have magically appeared, as I suddenly saw his smiling face. "It's all over," I whispered to him.

He didn't even hear me. He picked up the clipboard himself and read the same results aloud. Except, he added words. "Let's see, 80 percent of your left ovary is free from adhesions, and 60 percent of your right ovary is free also. We are a go for in vitro. Congratulations."

IVF in America

It was July 25, 1978, and would be a memorable one for the Drs. Howard and Georgeanna Jones. They had left their positions at Johns Hopkins Women's Clinic and were moving to Norfolk, Virginia, to begin working at the new Eastern Virginia Medical School. As they drove to Virginia from Baltimore, their friend Dr. Patrick Steptoe delivered Louise Brown, the world's first "test-tube baby," in England. At the same time, two Australian groups had been tirelessly working since 1973, in hopes that they would have the world's first IVF baby. Their baby girl was born in 1980, becoming the world's third test-tube baby, following two successful births in England.

I was leaving for Vancouver to have microsurgery by Dr. Gomel in November 1979, just three weeks after the Drs. Jones faced a crowded, six-hour meeting with proponents and very vocal opponents of their petition to the State of Virginia to open the first in vitro fertilization program in the United States. They were accused by protestors of "playing God."

I was in Hartford, Connecticut, having laser surgery on my right Fallopian tube in November 1980, as Georgeanne and Howard Jones sat puzzling over why they had not yet had a pregnancy in their new IVF program. Robert Edwards, a Cambridge scientist and partner of Dr. Steptoe, had worked with the Joneses at Johns Hopkins Medical School in 1965. They consulted with him via transatlantic phone calls and saw him when he visited the States. An endocrinologist, Dr. Georgeanne Jones decided not to heed Bob Edwards's warning against the use of ovary-stimulating drugs and began using the fertility drug Pergonal with their patients. This successfully resulted in more eggs ripening on the ovary each month, so that if one did not fertilize in vitro, there was a possibility that another would.

As Dr. Howard Jones wrote in his 2014 book, *In Vitro Fertilization Comes to America,* "One must recall that these were very early days for using a technology that is so widely familiar today."

I had undergone surgery five times and had lost both Fallopian tubes by December 28, 1981, when Elizabeth Jordan Carr was delivered at Eastern Virginia Medical School, making her "America's First Test-Tube Baby." The Joneses presented their research and history of their program in March 1982 at the American Fertility Society meeting in Las Vegas.

I entered the University of Texas Health Science's in vitro program in Houston, founded by Dr. Martin Quigley, in 1982, less than a year after Elizabeth Carr's birth. This was still a very early and experimental time period. The admiration and gratitude I have for the many scientists and physicians, working independently and collegially as they persevered despite failure and controversy to help women conceive their own babies, continues to grow to this day.

Chapter 17

"Ladies and gentlemen. We have just landed at Hobby International Airport. Enjoy your stay in Houston. And, thank you for flying Braniff."

I knew I was glowing. I was smiling so hard at the stewardesses and the other passengers that those who caught my eye smiled back as if they were confused that they might know me. I think I startled the captain in his seat in the cockpit as I said exuberantly, "Thank you," with a wave as I walked by the open cockpit door.

There was nowhere else on earth I would rather be right now than Houston in August. "Oh, my God, it is going to be a sauna," Cathy said the day before in her Southern drawl as she watched me lay a bathing suit in my suitcase. "You are crazy. People come from Texas to Colorado Springs for the summer to escape the heat. You are going the wrong direction."

But here I was, in Houston for my in vitro surgery, welcoming the heat as I walked outside the airport and waved at a driver sitting in the first taxi lined up along the curb. This thick air was concrete proof that I was really here. I was really going to have a test-tube baby.

The taxi dropped me under the portico of the Houston-Central Holiday Inn. I sighed. Last month, Peter and I had splurged and stayed at the fancy but old Shamrock Hilton. It was famous for being the largest hotel built in the 1940s. There were black-and-white photos on the walls of movie stars who had stayed there. The weekend before we flew to Houston, we rented the video movie *Giant* from a shop in Old Colorado City. It was a classic film starring Elizabeth Taylor, Rock Hudson, and James Dean. Some of the scenes showing the oil men's opulent lifestyle of Texas were filmed at the Shamrock hotel. We had gone into the jewelry shop off the lobby. Peter bought me a gold charm of an oil well. "We will strike oil here this time and get pregnant, I know it," he said.

I reached up and felt the charm hanging around my neck as I gazed at the simple hotel. This visit would be much longer; I was here for a week, alone, and Peter wouldn't join me until surgery was scheduled. We had to be economical. The hotel had been on a list given to us at the doctor's office as one that was close to the hospital and had daily shuttle transportation back and forth to the medical complex. I brushed my shoulder against an overgrown fiddle-leaf fig tree in the lobby as I lugged my suitcase to the front desk to check in. Then I walked up the outside stairs that had steel-colored, sparkly, grippy strips on the edge of each open step. It was so humid, and it probably rained often, making the steps slippery.

I bumped my suitcase up the steps behind me, one at a time, as a key, hanging from a green Holiday Inn fob with the numbers 256, bobbled in my other hand. I opened the door and entered a room with thick, olive-green curtains over the windows and a green faux-brocade bedspread on the double bed. The air conditioner rattled loudly. The bathroom toilet had a paper strip around the seat that said "Sanitized," and the drinking glasses by the sink wore pleated paper caps. I dropped my suitcase onto the bed with a bounce, but didn't have time to unpack. I had asked the desk clerk to call for another cab so I could get to the medical school in time for my appointment. I could see the yellow taxi already sitting, engine running, in front of the lobby doors as I moved the musty-smelling curtains aside to peek out. I locked the door of my room, popped the key into my purse, and held the metal railing as I ran back down the stairs.

I remembered seeing the signs for Hermann Hospital on the left and knew that the medical building with Dr. Quigley's office was across the street from the hospital. There was an enclosed walkway over the road connecting the two buildings. I paid the cab driver and I stood by myself waiting for the elevator.

"Are you scared?" Cathy had asked last week after I finished packing.

"Yes," I answered after a pause of two heartbeats. I purposely hadn't told anyone that every single surgery had scared me. It was terrifying to be alone in an operating room, seeing only the eyes of people's faces above their surgical masks. It was terrifying to be put under anesthesia, then awaken groggy and not knowing where I was or what had happened. It was terrifying waiting to learn if the surgery had been a success. But it was more terrifying to think that I might never have a baby. I knew exactly what I wanted and why I was doing this. I had to do it. I had to hold my chin up and be brave. I wanted a baby. More surgery was exactly what I had to do.

"Yes, I am scared," I'd told Cathy. "But that is not going to stop me."

I immediately recognized the pretty woman in a nurse's uniform who was smiling and walking toward me as I stepped into Dr. Quigley's waiting room. She was Sylvia Pace-Owens, to whom the doctor had introduced us following the laparoscopy that showed I could now be a candidate for in vitro fertilization. I remembered she was a nurse but with a higher level of training. She had been waiting for me to arrive today, and as we shook hands I felt as if I was arriving at someone's home, not a medical office. She seemed genuinely glad to see me. Sylvia led me through a door next to the desk where the young receptionist, who had said "Congratulations" to us, sat. Today she said, "Welcome back, Mrs. Casey," with the same smile. Sylvia had short, wavy, gray-blond hair; the shade Mother would have called platinum. She was tall and stood straight, exuding intelligence and the very appropriate importance of her role in the in vitro program. She was Dr. Quigley's link between himself and the patient. She was soft-spoken with that lovely soft diction of a Texan and looked me directly in the eyes.

"Now," she said with familiarity, "from now on you will come right through this door every morning into the back where all of us are. Don't even bother to check in at the front desk." The way she said "us" made me feel as if I was part of the group, part of the team. I felt a warmth inside my chest and up my neck. She guided me straight ahead to the nurses' station, and introduced me to Rose, a nurse who also seemed to be waiting to greet me.

"We are going to be friends," Rose said. "I will draw your blood every morning at the same time and walk it over to the lab myself to check your hormone levels for Dr. Quigley. We have our own lab right here." Her words told me she would take care of my blood, which seemed unusual and comforting at the same time. I felt as if I was in a safe and compact bubble in this office and that the people here all wanted to help me. Another nurse walked up to join her at the counter and affirmed to me that Rose could take blood without a patient even feeling it. I plopped down in a chair and Sylvia sat down next to me. She confirmed that I had taken Clomid, the prescribed fertility drug, daily, starting on Sunday, August 7th, through Wednesday, August 11th. Today was August 12th. The third nurse stood and chatted with us as a giant rubber band was tied tightly around my left upper arm. I looked down to see the blue veins on my inner arm bulge. The nurses asked me about leaving Peter in Colorado to work while I was here and wondered when he would arrive. They jokingly welcomed me to the experience of Houston's ninety-degree summer heat, and we all laughed after noticing we were all wearing cardigans to combat the freezing indoor air conditioning. I barely noticed the nurse, Rose, taking two vials of blood from my vein and was surprised to hear the elastic sound of the band already being removed from my arm. A Band-Aid was gently pressed onto my inner arm and I stood as the four of us turned to move in the same direction.

We all walked over to Dr. Quigley's office, where the door was open. Sylvia and I stepped in as the others stood smiling right behind us in the doorway. "So, you have had the first pinprick of many, I see," the doctor said warmly. "Sylvia will be your guide for the rest of the week, and you couldn't be in better hands," he added, nodding with genuine appreciation.

Sylvia then walked with me through the waiting room, out the office door, and back into the hall to the elevators. "I will be waiting every morning when you arrive to have your blood drawn," she said as my feelings of being alone began to fade. "Then, we will go together for your ultrasound. Now, remember, the more liquids you drink before you arrive tomorrow, the better your ultrasound will go. You need to drink at least four eight-ounce glasses before you arrive. Do not go to the bathroom, no matter what," she added with a smile.

I stopped at a small deli on the first floor, picked up a heavy paper plate with a rounded scoop of chicken salad sitting atop a piece of lettuce, looked wistfully at a bottle of Coke, but reached for orange juice instead. I wanted to be as healthy as possible before becoming pregnant. I took them to the cash register and paid. This would be dinner. I got into the first waiting cab outside the front doors and headed straight back to the hotel. Tomorrow I would start taking the shuttle bus, but today I just needed to be alone and get myself settled.

• • •

I ate my salad with a plastic fork while sitting on the edge of my hotel room bed, then tossed the plate into the small wastebasket. I put on my summer nightgown and wished I had brought flannel instead, as the air conditioning was freezing. I turned off the overhead light switch by the door and flipped on the table lamp. I leaned into the big pillow behind me and picked up my paperback.

"Believe in yourself!" was the first line. *The Power of Positive Thinking* was my choice for this special week. I had become completely immersed in Norman Vincent Peale's philosophy during the two-hour plane ride from Denver to Houston. The combination of faith and the mind/body connection was in perfect alignment with what I intended to create for myself. I believed in the power of training the mind for the good of my body and my attitude. I planned to apply this philosophy during my entire time in Houston and sat in bed, balancing the book on my raised knees, pen in hand to underline important sentences. I turned the lights off after reading, underlining, and rereading the perfect words, "Peace I leave with you, my peace I give unto you: not as the world giveth give I unto you. Let not your heart be troubled, neither let it be afraid."

I felt peaceful and calm as I slipped into sleep. That was exactly how I intended to live through the week.

Chapter 18

"**C**an I get you a little more coffee, honey?" I placed my left hand inside the book I was reading and looked up. The thin waitress, who smelled faintly of cigarette smoke, stood next to me with a pot of coffee. She looked too old to be a waitress and on her feet all day. Her skin reminded me of autumn corn husks. She had been here since I walked in at 7 this morning. She was wearing dangling copper earrings in the shape of a longhorn steer.

"Yes, please, and may I also have some more water?" I answered, smiling at her. She had already brought me one cup of coffee, two glasses of water, and a tall glass of orange juice. She leaned down and poured steaming coffee into my nearly empty mug. *I don't like drinking from thick institutional pottery*, I thought as I took a sip. I was sitting at a table beside the wall in a small restaurant at the Holiday Inn. There was a live yellow daisy in a tiny vase in the middle of the table. My mug sat on top of a white paper place mat with scalloped edges. She seemed to be the only waitress working. Only one other table was taken, by what looked like a worried middle-aged mother and her young adult daughter. The daughter was leaning halfway across the table and seemed to be trying to make a point to her mother.

Before I left my room this morning, I quickly chugged two glasses of water at the bathroom sink. I gulped each glass down without breathing between swallows. My target was to drink four eight-ounce glasses of liquids before I arrived at Hermann Hospital's medical offices this morning at 9. I intended to drink more, just to be safe. I am not quite sure why I needed such a full bladder but knew that it was important and necessary for the morning's ultrasound of my ovaries.

After drinking so much that my stomach felt distended, I stood inside the front door of the hotel to wait for the 8:30 shuttle bus to the hospital complex. I bumped the enormous fiddle-leaf fig tree with my purse again as I passed it. *That thing needs to be pruned,* I thought. *It is ridiculously leggy.* A minibus with the words "Texas Medical Center" over the front windshield pulled under the hotel portico right on time. I climbed up the two steps with a cheery "Good morning" to the driver. I noticed a step stool near his seat, probably to assist patients on and off. He stopped at other hotels along the way and picked up more passengers. Some of them looked really sick. "I am not sick," I assured myself and looked away, out the windows, as we continued along.

We drove through the huge medical complex. I had no idea it was so enormous with so many buildings, hospitals, and medical schools. The bus stopped at several hospitals to drop off passengers. I recognized the name of "MD Anderson" as the driver called it out. It was a well-known cancer hospital, and my full stomach suddenly lurched for the people who stood to get off. "But I am not sick," I reminded myself. I could see how this daily ride could get depressing, and I intended to stay positive.

I walked straight through the waiting room of Dr. Quigley's office to the door leading into the back rooms. I turned the doorknob firmly and pushed. I knew exactly where I was going after yesterday's visit. "Hi, Ellen," I was greeted warmly as I walked through the door by the two nurses I had met yesterday. Sylvia appeared next to me before I even got up to the nurses' station. It felt like when I walked into the teachers' lounge each morning and saw my colleagues. I noticed my tense shoulders relaxing in reaction to the comfort of being with people who seemed genuinely glad to see me. These weren't really my friends, but I was pretending, like a new girl on the first day of school, trying to slip in as a member of their group.

After Rose had drawn my blood from the same arm as yesterday, Sylvia walked with me back through the waiting room and out to the hall beyond. We turned away from the elevators as she asked, "Did you drink plenty of liquids this morning?"

"Yes, I sure did," I answered with a quiet laugh from deep in my throat, but stopped myself from adding, "and I desperately need to rush to the bathroom right now." My stomach no longer felt full with so much liquid, but my bladder was beginning to ache. I was steeled to go along with everything asked of me in this in vitro program, and to manifest a great attitude. I wanted every person involved in this process to like me. I still hoped that would help my chances of success. I had absolutely no power in this situation other than how I controlled my thoughts, attitude, and behavior. I was quite certain that the medical team would discuss how I was doing through this process emotionally, as well as medically, and I wanted only positive comments about me when they discussed my case. I looked quickly away as we passed the door marked "Ladies' Room."

Sylvia led me down the long hall, passing doctors' office doors listing names and specialties on wavy opaque glass. Then we turned a corner to enter the walkway that looked like a tube stretching between the medical building and Hermann Hospital, over the busy street below. We walked along next to each other like friends between classes in a school hallway. Sylvia talked all of the way. She explained that we were going over the bridge to the hospital and to the Radiology Department offices. I was on my way to have an ultrasound of my ovaries, which she had already prepared me for yesterday. There were no surprises in this in vitro journey so far and that put me at ease.

"You will love Dr. Maklad," she said. "He is the ultrasound specialist who will look at your ovaries every morning. He is a very important member of Dr. Quigley's team and was specially chosen. Dr. Quigley took great care to find only the best of the best for every aspect of his program," she said while opening a door under a Radiology Department sign. We did not even need to stop at the front desk but walked right past and through another side door. I felt like I had a backstage pass to a rock concert. I felt like a VIP.

Dr. Maklad's demeanor was calm and in control. I liked how his dry, warm hand felt when we shook hands in introduction. He cupped both of his hands around mine. I had been raised on the importance of a strong handshake and his exuded confidence. He moved across his large examination room to show me the ultrasound machine, something I had never seen. The only person I knew who had had an actual ultrasound was Cathy, and that was to confirm that she was carrying twins. "Let's get started right away," he said with a raise of his dark eyebrows. "I am going to guess that you would like to get this over as soon as possible and get to the nearest bathroom."

It felt like a risk to tell Sylvia that the pain in my bladder now felt dangerous. If they couldn't do the ultrasound because I couldn't hold thirty-two ounces of liquid in my bladder this morning, then I might be sent home. I just didn't know what might happen if I couldn't be brave enough to stand this pain. It was not at all the familiar sensation of needing to go to the bathroom by now; no, I was feeling desperate. By the time I was lying on the table with a clear, thick oil being smeared over my lower abdomen by a nurse, I was not just uncomfortable, but scared. It felt like lightning was shooting down my bladder walls in streaks. As Dr. Maklad moved a wand over the oily lotion and adjusted knobs on his machine, Sylvia distracted me by explaining that the full bladder pushed my ovaries high enough to the skin that the ultrasound machine could actually see the follicles, where the ova were developing. That was just astounding to me. I had no idea that these cavities could possibly be seen with ultrasound. Dr. Maklad read out numbers in millimeters five times, which both his assistant with a clipboard and Sylvia wrote down. "Wonderful, just wonderful," she confirmed, looking at me.

"Let me show you what I can see," he said, swiveling the screen of the ultrasound machine to face me. He outlined the ovary with his finger, then pointed at a black ovoid spot. "This is the follicle. An egg is growing inside of it. I can't see the actual egg but this shows me where it is ripening. It looks like your body is responding well to the hormones. Look at this." He moved the wand in a different direction. "There is another follicle." I focused on a second black spot. "Today I am taking measurements of each follicle as a baseline. Tomorrow when I look again, I will be able to monitor how each egg is growing by the change in size of the follicle."

The doctor nodded to his nurse. She wiped off my stomach thoroughly but gently, reached for my hand to pull me into a sitting position, and escorted me quickly to a bathroom just outside the examination room. As I sat on the toilet I leaned forward, elbows on my knees, and held my forehead heavy in my hands. It took some time before the sparks of pain in my bladder settled enough that I felt like I could walk back out the door.

I repeated the same routine the next morning. I again drank one more glass of liquids than required to at the hotel. I now had this one thing in my own control, and I was going to be successful in that. After yesterday's experience I knew that the sharp bladder pains were finite, and that I could and would make it through them by breathing deeply and relaxing. It was exciting on the second day to have Dr. Maklad congratulate me by saying, "Your egg follicles have grown by 4 millimeters. Yesterday they were at 12 and today they are 16. This is all good."

I smiled in response, hiding the fact that deep inside I was terrified. Halfway through the ultrasound, he had not been able to locate one of the follicles on the right ovary that he had seen and measured yesterday. He searched and searched, his wand moving with circular pivots of his wrist, leaning in closer to the screen and frowning. It was gone. I felt out of control of my body. What if each follicle began to collapse, with no egg growing? I felt an earthquake jolt my exam table, but no one else in the room reacted.

The doctor must have noticed a shadow pass across my face. "This has several possible explanations. Ovaries often change position. Also, one follicle can grow in the direction of another and push it out of sight of the scanner. You still have four good follicles growing."

But I felt a familiar vibration of fear in my diaphragm. I recognized my own physical reaction to loss. I was holding my breath.

Later I climbed up the stairs of the free shuttle back to the Holiday Inn and decided to spend some time at the pool. Holding a brown bottle of Coppertone, a towel, and *The Power of Positive Thinking*, I pushed down on the long metal bar and opened the door onto the pool area. It felt like walking into the Amazon jungle. The air was so thick, so humid, that I felt like I was suffocating. It was a shock to my lungs going in one breath from the icy air conditioning into total humidity. My hair was already curling— I knew without looking in a mirror—as I put my things down beside a lounge chair.

When Peter and I were in Tahiti for our honeymoon, I remember thinking that I was glad he hadn't seen my hair in humidity before we were married. My naturally curly hair is smooth in dry Colorado, but I turn into Shirley Temple in the tropics. By the Holiday Inn pool, I adjusted the chair back to a reclining position, put down my towel, lathered myself with Coppertone, and looked around the pool area. Only two other people were there. A father was tossing a little boy of about five as far as he could in the pool. Their low and high laughs joined together in the air like music. I smiled as I gathered my curls into a ponytail. The humidity was so high I felt as though I couldn't get a full breath. A round thermometer hanging off center on the pool fence read 95 degrees.

I picked up my book and began to read. The chapter was titled "A Peaceful Mind Generates Power." *Perfect*, I thought, and picked up my pen to begin underlining as I read. Near the end of that chapter, I was taken by lines describing feelings of guilt that lead to a state of constant apprehension. That state was familiar to me. I had lived in it for the past three years—terrified of my failure to conceive, of Peter stopping me from continuing my quest to have a baby because we couldn't afford it, and of rejection from the newest medical programs to give us our baby, since the day that very first blockage was discovered. I was always aware that I caused that tubal blockage by using an experimental IUD.

"Do I feel as if I deserve to be punished for having the IUD?" I wondered. Dr. Peale wrote, "Frequently I find that people who are lacking in inner peace are victims of a self-punishment mechanism. At some time in their experience, they have committed a sin and the sense of guilt haunts them. They have sincerely sought Divine forgiveness, and the good Lord will always forgive anyone who asks him and who means it. However, there is a curious quirk within the human mind whereby sometimes an individual will not forgive himself."

"Hmmm." I looked into the middle distance with a slight nod. "That is me." I continued to read on, acutely aware of a shift in my thoughts after reading that chapter. It was like my internal gyroscope had been slightly reset. Could I possibly be moving toward freedom from the omnipresent guilt of using the IUD that ruined my body? Perhaps I did not have to continue to be so fearful, so hard on myself.

Chapter 19

Alone. Completely alone. The frail woman across the aisle from me looked down at her hands, which were lightly folded over each other on her lap as we bumped along the road again this morning. I noticed her yesterday when she boarded the Medical Center shuttle. She looked about five years older than I was, certainly still in her thirties, but she had to pull herself up the two stairs of the bus, hand over hand, using the attached bar. Without speaking, she waved off the driver with a flip of the back of her hand when he lifted up the step stool and offered it to her. She wore a hand-fashioned turban made from a paisley scarf wound around and around her head. I was afraid that meant she was undergoing chemotherapy and losing her hair. It was confirmed when the bus stopped. She grasped tightly to the railing again and stepped back down the stairs slowly and carefully as she got off at MD Anderson Cancer Center.

Today she wore the same pretty scarf wrapped around her head. Its mélange of autumn colors offset her ashen skin. I remember the shock of horror when I saw myself, with skin drained of color exactly like hers was now, in an emergency room mirror the day my ectopic pregnancy ruptured. Her ears weren't covered, and I noticed tiny, gold hoops in each ear. The white tag on the back of her shirt was sticking up. I could hardly stand it for her. She was trying to look feminine, to hold on to her dignity, and this tag betrayed her efforts. I knew this young woman had gazed at her gray skin this morning in her hotel room mirror as she threaded in her pierced earrings and carefully drew soft pink lipstick on her colorless lips. I wanted to reach over and, with a whisper of a touch, tuck the tag back in for her. But I just couldn't bear it, for either of us.

I am so incredibly lucky. I quickly looked up to make sure that I hadn't said the words aloud but had held them safely inside as a thought. And then I chuckled, aloud this time, at my unspoken words. "I am so incredibly lucky" seemed laughably absurd when applied to my present reality of riding this jerking bus back and forth to the hospital every day in my last desperate attempt to get pregnant. All around me were people trying not to die. Regular people, just like me, were alone, completely alone, on this bus— existing in their own private permutations of hell. I thought of the play *Waiting for Godot* by Samuel Beckett that we read in ninth grade at Laurel and then saw performed at the downtown Cleveland Playhouse. *Theater of the Absurd*, I thought, looking around this bus. *I am living on that stage right now.* Nothing made any sense.

I reached down to twist my gold wedding band with its rows of tiny diamonds back and forth, back and forth. Yet my absurd thought was actually correct, although on a parallel plane to my condition during the past four years. I wasn't sick. I wasn't alone. Peter may have been in Colorado right now, but I had him. My mother wrote a letter to me each day addressed to the Holiday Inn on South Main Street in Houston, Texas. I had her. Long-distance calls were so expensive, so my friends in Colorado Springs called Peter daily to see how I was doing and told him to send me their love. I had them. My aunt Mary Ellen called from Cleveland to chat and two of my cousins got on the phone to buoy my spirits. I had my family. Every doctor who had ever tried to help me was there with me in spirit. And now, Dr. Quigley and his team were with me in every demonstrable way. They treated me as if I was working right along with them to achieve a pregnancy. We were all in this together. *I am so incredibly lucky*, I thought again, loudly inside my head.

Still, I couldn't shake the truth. It was really just me, suffering silently through this trauma alone and praying for redemption.

"Ow!" I winced involuntarily twenty minutes later. Unfolding my arm from bent to straight had just given me an unexpected and strangely deep pain. I had just stretched my left arm out to Rose, my "good friend," as she jokingly referred to herself, to have the rubber tourniquet tied around my upper arm so she could draw today's blood for the lab tests. I reflexively lay my warm right palm directly over the pain to soothe it away. When I finally lifted my hand away, I looked straight at Rose, sitting on a stool nearly touching my knee. She held my eyes just long enough, then looked away.

"Oh . . . ," she said in a long hum of genuine sympathy looking down now and gently touching my arm with her cool fingers, " . . . I know. Your poor vein must be really hurting by now. But, look at how beautiful it is!"

It was true. The inside crook of my arm, just three inches straight above my elbow, was the color of an oil slick. Each day, after a tube of blood was drawn, a new bruise bloomed. I now had shades varying from yellow, to reddish purple, to black, lying on top of each other.

"Beautiful," I responded with a sarcastic chuckle, looking away as I heard the rubber tie being snapped straight. I registered that I felt comfortable enough with this routine and this nurse that I didn't have to pretend to be so brave, and my response just now demonstrated that. We could laugh together and be serious together, and I relaxed into both. I was being enveloped into a warm comradery with every member of this very special team of Dr. Quigley's. I noticed they used the word "we" often. We all wanted the exact same result. Each day got easier. I was feeling more and more like myself.

"Good morning, Ellen," Dr. Maklad said, smiling at me as he came quickly across the ultrasound room to shake my hand. I was wearing a dress that I had made myself on my Singer sewing machine two years ago. It was a darling Liberty of London fabric with miniature blue and white flowers. Peter and I had gone to England a few months after my ectopic pregnancy. He indulged my excitement when I spotted the beautiful store and I ran in while he stood outside watching the busy street. I was thrilled to buy a few yards of Liberty of London's signature print fabric. My short dress was light and airy and I felt pretty. I packed it to wear outside in the Houston heat but discovered it was perfect for these days when I arrived at the hospital with a protruding stomach thanks to a bladder bursting with liquids.

"Ellen," Dr. Maklad said, "I have a favor to ask of you. Would you permit my wife to observe your follicular ultrasound today?" His eyebrows raised up high in punctuation to his question. "She is so excited that I get to work in the in vitro program, and she has never seen an ultrasound of the ovary. Would this be all right with you?"

A few minutes later, I felt like a bit of a star. Dr. Maklad's wife exclaimed, "Oh!" in a high burst of happiness as he pointed out my follicles. She stood peering over his shoulder, holding the back of his chair. As he pointed out each follicle, she would look away from the screen to nod and smile at me, then look right back at the screen. I was inexplicably proud that my eggs were growing. Yesterday, the ultrasound had spotted the follicle that was missing the day before. I was so relieved. All five follicles were visible again today.

"Look at this," Dr. Maklad said with a quiet excitement in his tone. He swiveled the screen to face me as I lay on my back with my stomach bared and slicked with thick oil. He carefully pressed his wand over my right ovary. "Do you see this cloudy cumulus inside of the black follicle?" He used his finger to point out a foggy area over the black circle of the follicle on the screen. I stared at the screen without blinking. "That is the actual ovum. It is really exciting to see one."

"Wow," I said, turning to share this with Sylvia, who stood next to me as she did through every morning exam. She was leaning in, staring at the picture intently.

"Wow is right," she said softly. Every smiling face in the ultrasound room was jutting forward, staring at the screen.

"Wait," cautioned the doctor with a smile and a finger raised. He turned some knobs with intent and then snapped an instant photo of the elusive cumulus from inside the ultrasound machine. I couldn't believe the machine could do such a thing. It was like he had laid a gold coin in my palm when he turned and handed the instant photo to me. I stared at it. I treasured it. This photo made everything real. I now knew without a doubt that the follicles were actually holding eggs. I held concrete proof in my hand. I wanted to whoop, I was so excited. Now Peter could actually see what I had been trying to describe to him over the phone each evening.

"Let's let Ellen run to the bathroom to empty her bladder, and then I want to talk with you both," Dr. Maklad said to Sylvia as the grease was being wiped off my abdomen with a white towel.

A grinning Dr. Maklad walked across the room with an outstretched arm to shake my hand and thank me for letting his wife observe. "We did it!" he exclaimed. Sylvia and I stood side by side facing the doctor. I was the only one not wearing a starched white medical coat. "Your follicles have reached 20 mm, and that is our target size."

I turned to look at Sylvia for a reaction.

"Perfect," she said elegantly.

Suddenly, I felt as excited as I ever had in my quest to have a baby. My eggs were ready. I wished desperately that I could have a private moment in a room alone, to dance like a football player in the end zone after just scoring a touchdown, then walk back out totally composed. I was trying now to project calmness and stood up taller. I guessed that appearing overly optimistic might concern Sylvia and the IVF team, as the odds of success were still so small.

I flashed back to a memory of having this same excited feeling and being unable to show it. I was sitting at my gate in the International Terminal at O'Hare exactly ten years earlier. It was my first trip to Europe. I had saved every extra dollar from my first-year teaching salary of $670 a month to pay for the adventure. Evie and I were on the floor leaning against a wall, waiting for the plane. She was reading *Europe on 5 Dollars a Day*, and I was enjoying observing the other people in the lounge area. I especially noticed some hippie-looking couples who were sitting on the floor and looked around our age. I watched a family of four traveling together, each carrying an expensive khaki trench coat. They were sitting in adjoining chairs but not speaking to each other very often. There was a cute daughter with a short haircut, who looked as if she, like us, had just graduated from college in the past year or two. Her air of ennui made the pronounced point that she was totally unimpressed at preparing to board a plane to Rome. I deduced she had either already traveled in Europe and this trip was not special to her, or she was disdainful at having to travel with her parents and younger brother.

By contrast, I could feel my own heart fluttering wildly with excitement as I tried to stop smiling so hard. I couldn't believe Evie and I had so meticulously planned this entire trip and that I actually would get to see the Parthenon, the Pantheon, the Little

Mermaid statue. I wanted to jump to my feet and shout, "I am going to Europe!" But then, to blend in to this crowd of travelers, I worked to put on an air of studied nonchalance. But that joyous bubble of anticipation percolated in my chest.

That same bubble was right back inside me on that hot Houston morning as I walked next to Sylvia through the halls of the hospital. Again, I was trying to pull a sophisticated mask over my thrilled self and held my hands in fists to quell my desire to jump up and down and shout.

Before we reached the tunnel to cross over to the medical building, Sylvia guided me into a quiet laboratory waiting room. She motioned for me to take a seat. Always poised, she sat in the chair next to me, and balanced right on the outside edge of her seat, so that she was practically facing me. Sylvia held her hand on top of a folder full of papers, a bulging mailing envelope, and a clipboard in her lap. She stared straight and calmly into my eyes. I knew I could trust her after spending every day together this week—as she gently guided me through halls, stayed next to me in exam rooms, and answered my questions. Now, she carefully explained that we were at the stage in this in vitro fertilization process where the embryologist becomes important. He would be making a culture medium from my own blood in which the embryos would rest. I silently thanked my high school biology teacher for having us do experiments with cultures in petri dishes. I could picture exactly what she meant. A door opened and in walked a man in a lab coat. He shook hands with Sylvia then turned to me.

"Mrs. Casey, I am Dr. Don Wolf. I am the lab director here as well as the embryologist who will care for your embryos." Dr.

Wolf sat on the other side of me. Sylvia and I were rapt as he spoke using such beautifully descriptive words. I listened intently as he explained in detail every step that would occur in his lab after my eggs were aspirated—a technique using a laparoscopically inserted needle to remove each egg from the ovarian follicle—by Dr. Quigley and then delivered into his care.

Every single bit of this information was completely new to me, as there was no information anywhere explaining exactly what happened after an egg was fertilized. This was an experimental process and in constant flux. All the public heard, which was very little, was that the egg was fertilized in a lab. No one really thought or talked about how that actually happened.

I only knew of four other women in the world who'd had the in vitro procedure. One was the mother of the very first test-tube baby, Louise Brown, in England; a second one from that same program of Dr. Steptoe's; one in Australia; and Judy Carr, the mother of the first test-tube baby born in the US. As far as I knew, there had been no other births. There had been absolutely no way to learn the specifics until that very moment.

Now, I was hearing minute details. I focused on his every word—describing exactly where fertilization occurs and what happens next. My fertilized embryos would be kept in Dr. Wolf's lab in a warm, temperature-controlled machine, inside of which were metal racks. I visualized a refrigerator-like appliance with heating coils instead of cooling apparatus. The door would remain closed so the embryos would be in pitch dark, just as they would be in the womb. The embryos would only be carefully removed and placed under a microscope once a day so Dr. Wolf could observe the progress of their essential cell division. The temperature would be maintained at 98.6 degrees, again to approximate conditions inside of my womb. Each embryo would be in its own shallow petri dish, covered with a lid, and would be carefully numbered and marked with my name. He emphasized the extreme care he would take in handling my embryos, which we each knew were hopefully my future babies. Dr. Wolf was thorough in his explanations, clearly competent; and his choice of words like "caring for" and "carefully" conveyed an emotional connection. I was certain he would do his absolute best. I felt buoyed by the sense that he strongly shared my hope that one of Peter's and my embryos would blossom into a viable pregnancy. A pregnancy would be his success as well. He held my hand tightly in both of his as we shook hands again. I breathed out audibly and felt a smile lift my cheeks.

Dr. Wolf had clearly explained the special medium he would create in which my ovum and Peter's sperm would meet and where the fertilized embryo would grow. He said he had talked with the embryologists in London and in Norfolk to discuss what permutations of the culture had been successful. We walked through a door into the front room of his lab. Sylvia drew the four vials of my blood that would be used as the culture. It occurred to me later that evening, back in my hotel room, that I had not even reacted to my fragile, tender vein being stabbed again with a needle.

I peered through a glass window into the impressive embryology laboratory. The worker I spotted inside was completely covered from head to toe. He was dressed like the sinister government expert examining the tiny alien hero in the just-released movie *E.T.* I assumed that this protective garb was to maintain a sterile environment, something I had only seen in the movies. I admired and appreciated how this embryology facet of Dr. Quigley's in vitro program was working scientifically to approximate the environment of natural fertilization inside my actual body. It made such sense that the medium holding my embryos be created from my own blood.

After being able to view the pristine lab through the windows, I left feeling devoid of anxiety, which always seemed to result from not knowing something important to me. I felt I understood this crucial stage in the in vitro process now, and relaxed.

This is so cool, I thought as Sylvia opened the door for me to pass back through. I remembered that Peter once said to me, "Do you know that your highest praise for something is that it is *cool?*" I was a child of the 1960s, and being a part of this in vitro program did deserve a superlative. It was, indeed, very cool.

Sylvia guided me to a soft oatmeal-colored couch in the empty laboratory waiting room and we both plopped down. The cushions puffed out air. It was so nice to flop back onto the pillow behind me. My brain needed a momentary respite from concentration. Sylvia placed some of her armful of paperwork out of sight on the couch behind her. She laid a folder on her lap, along with a bulging mailing envelope. It was the same kind of envelope we used to send filmstrips between schools and the AV department in my school district.

First, she opened the folder and handed me several typed pages. "Dr. Quigley and I want you to know exactly what comes next, now that your egg follicles have reached 20 mm in size. First of all, you'll be glad to know that you don't have to go for an ultrasound tomorrow morning."

"Oh," I said, "I'll miss Dr. Maklad. I really like him. On the other hand, maybe I will have room for breakfast now that I won't have to drink all of those liquids!"

She smiled and continued. "The top page gives you directions to the lab where you and Peter will deliver his sperm the morning of your laparoscopy, two days from today. I will show you exactly where that laboratory is in a few minutes. It's easy to find, but you will both be excited the morning of the procedure and it helps to have a map in hand when maneuvering through the hospital."

I slipped that stiff paper under the other to see a new set of instructions.

"The next page is the hospital consent form for your laparoscopy, which you can sign and bring along with you in the morning. If you leave it in your room by mistake, do not panic."

How did she know I was a perfectionist, prone to panic over neglected details? I felt a wave of worry. Then I realized it would make sense that she was indeed very aware how much drive it had taken to get myself into this new program. I suspect that she also knew my determined history of researching other top fertility physicians in the preceding years. Her soothing words about not needing to panic actually would alleviate my stress the morning of my surgery.

A breeze of a thought whispered in my mind: *Did the in vitro program have a psychologist working with them to carefully craft the medical team's behavior, specific word usage, and doling out of information?*

Sylvia continued. "Late tonight, you will come back to the hospital to have blood drawn. Then, you will be given an injection of hCG, which is the acronym for a man-made biochemical compound called human chorionic gonadotropin. Each month, the female pituitary gland produces and secretes a hormone we call luteinizing hormone, LH for short. That hormone triggers ovulation. Scientists have created hCG to mimic the effect of your body's own LH. I know you, Ellen, and you are already wondering why we are giving you a shot instead of letting your body secrete its own hormone."

She smiled. "Here's why. We have to precisely time the laparoscopy for the aspiration of your eggs. It is imperative that surgery happens *before* you ovulate." She strongly emphasized the word "before." I totally understood this point; if ovulation has occurred, there would be no eggs to retrieve. Sylvia looked to me seriously to see if I needed any further explanation. I nodded in a "yes, I have got it" gesture and she continued.

"Now, here is everything you need for tonight," she said, opening the stuffed envelope. First, she held up a small box. When she opened it, I saw a small vial with a blue and white label on it.

"This is the hCG for your injection tonight." She replaced both the box and tubes into the envelope and pulled out a new typed paper. She held one side and I held the other as we bowed heads to read the words together. A passerby might have considered that we were praying together.

I was to go to Hermann Hospital's Labor and Delivery Department and ask for the head nurse, who would be expecting me. I needed to have the hCG injection as close to 11 PM as possible. She explained that thirty-six hours after that shot, ovulation would occur. My egg aspiration would be two hours before ovulation. After so many years of taking my basal temperature each morning to try to roughly predict my own ovulation, this new understanding of its exact timing astounded me intellectually. A brilliant collective of scientists and medical doctors had been intensely studying the specifics of human reproduction with the goal that I, and other women just like me who could not conceive naturally, might be able to give birth to our very own babies. I was speechless at the weight of this magnificent realization.

"Oh, I am sorry," I quickly said, upon realizing that Sylvia was waiting for me to look at the next sheet she was holding. "I am just so thrilled by the caliber of research that has been done here. This is just a medical wonder. I am in awe. Thank you."

I smiled at her with genuine gratitude. She reached over and squeezed my hand.

The new sheet held typed instructions for the head nurse, which I would present to her that night. Sylvia returned all the papers to the full envelope and passed it to me with a silent nod to its importance. I clasped it protectively against my chest in what felt just like a hug. I would be certain to arrive exactly on time tonight. No, I would arrive earlier.

• • •

The elevator doors opened with a metallic gasp. Sylvia and I stepped in. Glancing around quickly, I remembered that the gargantuan size of hospital elevators always took me by surprise. The elevator wasn't even half full. A gurney carrying a sedated patient attached to an IV pole was in the far back, attended by a nurse and an orderly, both staring straight ahead. A woman wearing a blue suit with an official hospital name tag stood next to two silent men. The younger man was carrying a duffel bag. The slight scent of Shalimar floated off the woman in the blue suit as I moved into place near her. No one looked at us. So many people were in this one elevator and still there was no sound or even movement. "Everyone is pretending that no one else is here," I thought as I saw eyes focused on nothing, staring straight ahead at the closing doors.

We exited the elevator on the lowest floor. It didn't feel like we were even in a hospital anymore once we got off. The walls and floors were tiled and it made me think of an indoor swimming pool hallway. A large sign said "Laundry." I smelled the hot odor of ironing. Sylvia and I turned away from the sign and I saw that we were entering a tunnel.

"This is the tunnel that connects the medical school to Hermann Hospital," Sylvia explained, gesturing ahead with an upturned palm. It was brightly lit as we began walking through to the far side. "Tuesday morning, you and Peter will deliver his sperm specimen to the medical school."

We stepped into another elevator and rode in silence to the second floor, where I was introduced to yet another critically important member of the in vitro team, Dr. Sokolow. He was a sperm scientist and obviously had to have a sense of humor when he introduced himself as such. "Most people are wary to shake my hand," he joked as I extended mine. His comment had embarrassed me, instead of putting me at ease, and I felt my face turn scarlet. He was upbeat and animated and seemed quite excited to do his part for us on Tuesday.

"Could you please explain to me exactly what it is you do?" I asked seriously. Peter's sperm in this process was a detail I had never even thought about specifically, and I was slightly ashamed. I assumed it was just poured into the petri dish with an ovum. My lack of knowledge, again, was the result of the complete dearth of public information on this new, and constantly changing, experiment called in vitro fertilization. The embryologist had explained his part earlier today, and now the sperm technician did exactly the same, clearly detailing his scientific role.

Dr. Sokolow explained that the sperm had to be washed, meaning that the seminal fluid is completely removed so that the sperm are in a liquid rather than natural thick gel. Then, it is kept in an incubator at body temperature until the eggs are ready for fertilization.

"I am honored to be a part of helping you and your husband," he said, holding my hand and giving it a squeeze that seemed to say "I am in this with you" as we said good-bye. His eyes crinkled at the edges as he smiled and his head nodded up and down in a "yes." Tears suddenly threatened to flood my eyes in a surprise reaction to his sincerity. Here was yet another member of Dr. Quigley's team making an effort to make me feel so welcome, so special. I exhaled out all but a tiny lump of my remaining anxiety.

With Sylvia by my side, like a good friend, we walked back to Hermann Hospital. I saw that Labor and Delivery was on the second floor when I looked at a sign by the elevators showing all the medical departments. Sylvia walked me past the elevators and over to the emergency room entrance that was kept open at all hours. I would come in through this door tonight, she told me.

"Be sure to tell your taxi driver to wait right here for you. You won't be inside for more than fifteen minutes." Mother always frightened me when she said that hospitals were dangerous places to be alone, especially outside in the parking lots or inside in stairwells, so I knew exactly why Sylvia specified this.

A terrible, overpowering memory popped right into my vision and absorbed me instantly. I was transported back to a few years earlier, standing stunned, next to my unexpectedly ill mother's hospital bed in Bridgeport, Connecticut.

"Ellen, take off that necklace. You are just asking to be attacked in the parking garage," she'd said sharply. I reached up and wrapped my fingers around the detailed gold coin set in a bezel that my then-boyfriend had given me. I took my hand away from the necklace and looked away from my mother.

Her husband had died very suddenly at age fifty, and it wasn't until I married Peter years later that I realized how impossible it would be to continue breathing without the man who was your oxygen. She barked orders at me as a result of physical pain and from the worse pain of overwhelming grief at losing her love. I wore my gold coin in protest to being told what to do at age twenty-five. Still, I did feel a zinging current of panic in my stomach and whipped my head right and left looking around the hospital parking garage as I walked to and from my car that week.

"Thank you, Sylvia," I responded. "I promise to have the taxi wait."

Late that evening a yellow taxi pulled up in front of the Holiday Inn. I watched the driver lean down to peer through the passenger window into the small lobby, so I waved as I pushed the door open into the sticky July night air. The humidity hit me like a wall. If there had been five more degrees of humidity, I would have been breathing in pure water. I hopped into the cab and shut the door hard behind me. The driver had his arm stretched over the back seat and looked at me.

"Where to?"

"Hermann Hospital, please. Emergency entrance." I saw the look on his face. "No, no, don't worry," I laughed lightly. "Nothing is wrong. I am just going in for a quick thing. Nothing is wrong, I promise." I didn't want him to be concerned, but neither did I feel the need to explain why exactly a woman alone was traveling to the Emergency Department at 10:30 PM.

Houston felt very different, driving through it at night. A cloudy sky was glowing strangely, reflecting the city lights off in the distance. There was hardly any traffic on this Sunday. The driver and I remained silent.

Spotlights at Hermann Hospital shone up toward palm trees lined on the circular driveway leading to the emergency entrance, giving the appearance of a fancy hotel. Sirens split the air as an ambulance raced around us to the automatic doors. My driver pulled up slowly and we waited as the patient was unloaded in a flurry of activity and wheeled into the building. I was relieved the taxi air conditioner was loud enough that we could not hear any urgent voices.

"I am only running in for a quick blood test," I explained. "Can you please wait for me and take me back to the hotel?" I probably should have thought to ask him this before we left the Holiday Inn, I worried. "I don't like being out here alone at night."

"No problem, miss," he answered slowly, as if he'd heard this request before. "I will pull up right to there." He pointed ahead to a darker curb just past the brightly lit entrance.

"Perfect," I said gratefully. "I absolutely promise that I will come back out. Please keep your meter running so that I can pay you for your time waiting," I added. I needed to know that he would be there when I came out. Worry buzzed in my ears.

"I will wait right up there, ma'am," and he pointed again. I just had to trust him, I thought, as I jumped out of the car and said I would see him soon.

Tonight was the very first time Sylvia wouldn't be waiting to greet me and guide me. I pushed my shoulders down and held my head high. I had learned over years of entering new medical buildings that good posture gave me confidence. Thanks to Sylvia's tour earlier today, I knew just where I was going. I walked up a flight of stairs and through the back entrance of the Labor and Delivery Department. The door said "Employees Only," and opening it gave me a burst of importance and a memory of our backstage passes at a Huey Lewis and the News concert. The private door opened to a surprisingly quiet nurses' area. It was separated from any patients, which was a bit of a relief to me. I had been dismayed when I was told I had to go to the Labor and Delivery Department.

I already steeled myself for what I might encounter on this floor. I feared being overwhelmed by the chaotic sounds of women in labor and joyful exclamations of delight after delivery. I was worried about how I might emotionally react to being among these women who had everything I wanted so badly. They were all about to become mothers. As I stepped into this unexpectedly calm, controlled atmosphere, I felt my mind release my fear. I had prepared for a scary circumstance I would not have to face tonight. Before I could even enter the office area, a woman with a big smile approached, as if expecting me.

"Are you Dr. Quigley's lucky patient?" she asked, glancing at the fat folder I was clutching protectively to my chest. I liked the sound of that word, "lucky." Every day this week confirmed exactly how lucky I was to be an in vitro candidate. I also felt acknowledged, many times, for the tenacity it took for me to be one of the first patients accepted into this very new program.

She introduced herself as the head nurse, and we walked toward a nearby room. She closed the door behind us with a click. I handed her the envelope, which she opened. She very carefully read every word of the typed note.

"Okay," she said brightly. "Let's draw your blood first. Then, I will give you the injection of hCG you just delivered to me in this little box." She held up the box. There was a knock on the door and another nurse entered apologetically with a quietly spoken question. "I will be right with you in a few minutes," my nurse said. "This special lady gets my full attention right now." She turned back to me with a smile. My left arm really hurt deeply again as I stretched it out for another drawing of my blood. I glanced down toward the pain and saw that my bruising was even more intense than it had been that morning. I now draped a cardigan over my shoulder everywhere I went so no one would be shocked at my poor arm's appearance.

Moments later, I felt my glutes clench in reaction to the shot administered very deeply into my left hip. My muscles clenched like they were clamping right around the needle, trying to stop its descent.

"There you go," the nurse said as she massaged the place where the needle had been to loosen my muscles. As we left the room and walked to the staircase door together, she said, "Best of luck to you, Mrs. Casey." Her body moved slightly and it seemed like she wanted to hug me. The look in her dark eyes, as she helped me push the heavy door open, held anticipation, as if we were getting ready to walk into a great party together. A tiny flash of excitement rushed up my spine.

Only ten minutes after I had stepped out of it, I knocked on the window of the cab. I sighed in relief that the driver was waiting just where he said he would be. Green and white dots of light sparkled on his running radio. He turned the knob off with a flick of his wrist as I opened the door and got in. I was wearing a sundress and cardigan and felt my thighs settle onto the sticky vinyl seat. "Thank you so much for waiting for me," I said. "Thank you."

Thank you, thank you, thank you, I thought. *Thank you, driver, thank you, God, thank you, nurses, thank you, doctors, thank you, scientists, thank you, Peter.*

• • •

The next day back at the hotel, after having blood drawn once again in the hospital by Rose, my quick, shallow breathing alerted me that I was overly excited.

I knew I had a brilliant and unique reason to be this excited. Here I was in Houston, one of the very first women to go through this experimental in vitro fertilization process in the United States—actually, one of the first in the world. The potential for success was stunning. I really could have our own baby.

I dove into the lukewarm pool and swam some laps to calm myself down physically. I focused on the wide navy line running the length of the pool bottom. Then I rested, chin on my arms folded on the tiled ledge, and breathed slowly. I scooped up a beetle that floated past on its back. I had continued reading my book about positive thinking and consciously tried to control my attitude, to remain calm and positive. But learning that my eggs were ripe and knowing now that the ovum aspiration surgery, followed by the actual in vitro fertilization, would be in just a day and a half had me dancing up the stairs and back to my room for a long warm shower. After a light dinner of a gazpacho, a side salad, and tea, I hopped into bed to read. I felt calm and focused.

Yipes, this is my last day alone in Houston, I thought the next morning as I sat on the Medical Center shuttle bus. Peter would arrive from Colorado later that night. Tomorrow was the big day, the day when I would have the in vitro fertilization procedure— when they would harvest my eggs, fertilize them with Peter's sperm, and place the embryos into the lab incubator.

Today, I knew that all I had to do was go to Dr. Quigley's office to have Rose draw her last vials of blood. I wouldn't need another ultrasound. Yet today's blood test was of enormous importance, and I almost wished Sylvia hadn't explained it to me.

"Your blood hormone levels will be tested in our lab to see if you have ovulated," Sylvia told me as Rose drew the first vial of blood. "If ovulation has occurred, I will call you this evening and we won't be able to proceed with the egg aspiration in the morning."

I froze in my chair. The familiar panic of impending loss paralyzed me. *Oh, my God, what if we couldn't try in vitro tomorrow after all?* I unconsciously held my breath. There was nothing I could think of to say, even if my strangely tingling lips had been able to form words in this cold state of terror. Everything around me was fading into gray. My ears felt suddenly plugged and unable to hear. A muffled roaring in my ears sounded like I was cupping both palms over them.

A cool hand was placed over mine. "Are you feeling okay?" Sylvia asked. I nodded but couldn't speak any more words. I was wondering if this was how a person felt right before fainting.

"I'm okay," I heard my quiet, low voice reply. I noticed I was trembling all over and held my hands together so she wouldn't notice. A glass of water was placed in my hands and I sipped it without thinking.

"I think I upset you just now when I discussed the possibility of ovulation before surgery," she said gently. "Here is what I think just happened. You were holding your breath and didn't have enough oxygen. This is a good thing for you to remember when you are in as stressful a situation as you have been in this week. Breathe. Breathe. Breathe."

I nodded and inhaled.

"Ellen, you have been so brave, so upbeat, so positive. Each member of Dr. Quigley's team has remarked at our daily meetings about your incredibly sunny attitude. We know that this is hard for the patients. You have worked to maintain such an important, positive manner of handling all of the stresses and physical discomfort; you've been our star patient. I don't want you to worry about having already ovulated. It is such a minute possibility, but it is important for you to understand every aspect of your program beforehand." I nodded again in agreement.

"You must be excited that your husband arrives tonight." She smiled, and slowly I was able to return to our comfortable, normal conversational pattern. "Now, let me answer any questions that you have about your big day tomorrow. Even if you think the question is silly, please ask it anyway."

"Oh, you have been so wonderful giving me every little bit of information," I said, lifting my eyes up to the ceiling, thinking. "I really can't think of anything else. That's amazing for me, as I always have questions, right?"

We laughed at the same time.

"Well, then," Sylvia tipped her head to the side and settled me with such a warm, loving look, "I will see you and Peter in the morning."

I glided out the office door that Sylvia held open for me, floating along on a stream of calm. It had been cathartic to feel that moment of panic and to get through it. I now felt relaxed and mildly euphoric. I was awash in that same smooth feeling I have when I am engrossed in making one of my pen-and-ink drawings and when I am skiing to the bottom of the slopes at the end of a winter day. It is exactly how I feel every time I hold a tiny baby in my arms.

It is the pure understanding that everything is right with my world. I am going to do this.

Chapter 20

The light turned red and our taxi stopped. Two joggers in nylon shorts ran by on the road, sweating and shouting to each other to be heard over the light morning traffic. Peter and I had agreed it was best to take a taxi to the hospital this morning. I was anxious about arriving late if the free shuttle didn't pull up to the lobby doors exactly on time; I needed a smooth, calm morning and couldn't leave anything to chance.

It was still early, and the Houston heat hadn't quite yet filled the shadows, but humidity already glistened in dotted beads of moisture on every veined leaf and every blade of grass. A lady watered her lawn with a green hose as a yellow cat rubbed its back against her porch, wrapping its tail around the railing. A long, empty school bus passed us, going in the opposite direction.

I gazed out at the easy pattern of this morning as I watched people going about their daily routines, unaware of the reproductive technology taking place in a hospital just a few miles away. What might they think if they knew I had a container of sperm in a bag in my purse?

I glanced at Peter sitting on my right. I was always startled by how handsome he was. We had been married now for three years and I still had such a crush on him that I flushed just looking at him. I smiled at his wavy black hair, still wet from the shower. He had it cut yesterday before flying down to Texas. His stockbroker colleagues called him "Senator Casey" when he arrived at work looking so dashing after seeing his barber. He felt my eyes on him and turned. I know he saw me smiling.

"Everything okay over there?" he asked wryly.

I laughed in appreciation of his typical dry humor. There we were, on our way to the hospital for my sixth surgery. "Everything is great," I responded and paused before adding, "actually, I'm excited. Well, I am not excited about surgery, obviously, but I am excited that by this time tomorrow we might actually have embryos." I shook my head in disbelief. "I have gotten to live right in the middle of this scientific experiment all week. It is absolutely amazing that we are a part of it. It was like I was an exotic creature existing in a terrarium where each rock had been placed perfectly, each plant carefully chosen, the light set at just the correct temperature, all just for me. It was like being in a biosphere where everyone was working together for the same results. And that result is a baby for the two of us."

"It's all because of you," Peter said, "that we are here. I am really proud of you." He was so spare with his words, I caught this glowing compliment with open hands and held on to it. There is no one on earth whose praise I would be more honored to receive. I admired everything about Peter Casey. He studied constantly, reading biographies, philosophy, religion, and classics. From the first day I spotted him alone in the Hutton office, still working after everyone else had started their Friday afternoon drinking in the downstairs bar, through the past three years where he had often gotten out of bed at 2 AM to scratch notes about specific stocks ideas that had come to him in the middle of the night, I had been impressed by his drive. I was so glad that he was in this with me. I was relieved he was finally here in Houston.

I looked back out the window at a young woman sitting on her front steps in shorts, resting a coffee cup on her bare knee and looking at the passing cars. I wondered what she would do with her day today. The front screen door opened behind her and a sleepy-looking blond man, probably her husband, held it open with his shoulder as he scooped cereal slowly from a bowl. She turned her head to look up at him. I wondered what they would think if they knew what my day was going to be like. If I said "test-tube baby" to them, would they picture a baby growing in a jar in a laboratory? Would they look at each other and ask, "Isn't that science fiction?"

The light turned green and I was pressed back into the seat as the car moved forward toward the medical complex. I felt a quick lightness in my stomach, like when an airplane drops in altitude. I was trying to remain tranquil, in disciplined self-control today, but it was not easy.

As we pulled up to the medical school adjoining Hermann Hospital, a chilly thrill rushed across my skin, leaving a million duck bumps in its wake. The results of today's surgery had only two possible outcomes for me: abject joy or absolute devastation.

It was early, so there were only a few people walking purposefully around the usually busy area as we stepped out of the cab and walked onto the concrete plaza. All of our doctors and nurses—the anesthesiologist and embryologist, surgeon, nurse practitioner, and sperm lab scientist—must already be inside the hospital, I realized with a thrill zipping up my spine. They probably had to be ready well before Peter and I arrived.

"Now what? You're in charge." Peter's words snapped me out of my thoughts. I didn't hear him pay the driver but now noticed the back of our taxi driving away.

I tipped my chin up to gaze at the building Sylvia and I had visited the day before yesterday. Everything felt still. It felt like I was moving in slow motion through a Salvador Dalí landscape. Everything was soft-edged, disappearing behind me as I passed. Normal sights—a rectangular bed of begonias, the flagpole, even the pattern of bricks on the building façade—all seemed on a different plane from mine. We walked forward toward the wide revolving doors.

Today really was "the day." There had been so many doctors, so many surgeries, so many losses. I had felt comfortable all week in Houston but today everything mattered.

Today was either the end or the beginning of my dream.

I held up a small piece of paper that was damp from being clenched tightly in my hand. Slightly blurred ink said "Dr. Sokolow" and listed his floor and the number of the lab. We rode the elevator up and exited on his floor. I couldn't think of a thing to say to Peter. My heart was pounding so hard inside my chest that I knew I would see it if I looked down at my dress.

We entered the small lab sitting area. "Good morning. Peter and Ellen Casey for Dr. Sokolow," I said to the receptionist. "We have something to give him."

"Something." Normally Peter would have cracked a joke at my use of a euphemism, but I think he felt nervous, too. He held his neck long and straight, reminding me of why he had been given the family nickname "Goose."

Dr. Sokolow walked out to greet us. He must have been close by and heard my voice saying we were here to see him, as the receptionist hadn't even turned around yet to look for him. He opened the door and walked out into the waiting room to greet us, smiling as if we were the only people in the world he wanted to see today. It was like seeing the father of the bride effusively welcoming guests to the church before the wedding.

I handed him the paper bag, pulled from my purse, after he shook hands in introduction with Peter. Up until today, Peter had only met Dr. Quigley and Sylvia, so I was glad this special scientist was so excitedly anticipating his role today on the in vitro fertilization team. I noticed he put Peter at ease.

"Best of luck to you," he said to us both. He clapped a hand on Peter's shoulder briefly.

"Thanks," we said at the same time.

"No, seriously, thanks a lot," Peter added sincerely, turning back to look at the doctor with a nod. He actually really was in this with me today, I realized with a start. His tone of voice made me turn around to look back at him. This was the very first time in all of these years trying to have a baby that Peter actually got to play a role, other than just kissing me good-bye as I was being rolled into yet another operating room.

I wondered what he was thinking right now. I wondered if being physically involved himself this time, with his sperm now at a cutting-edge laboratory, made him feel more a part of what I was going through. Did this make the chance for our child more concrete to him? Was he full of hope, too, this morning? I wondered, but I didn't ask. I would discuss this with him in some future time when I was finally pregnant, I thought, but not today. I could not bring up his feelings right now, while we were still floating in limbo, like a bride and groom in a Chagall painting.

"Okay, that's over, now where do we go?" Peter sounded relieved as we waited at the silver doors for the down elevator. He wiped his glasses clean on a handkerchief.

It is all up to me now. I switched my train of thought totally and slowly took a long, deep breath. I had to concentrate inward, on my mindset, and my body. I was determined to keep my body calm. I was doing everything I could to block out the voice in my head that had just popped up and was bedeviling me with worries that my eggs had dissolved.

I was so relieved when I awoke at dawn that morning and realized that Sylvia hadn't called the night before to tragically report that my blood test showed I had already ovulated. I kept looking at the phone on the bedside table all evening, terrified that it would ring. I stared hard at the receiver, willing it to stay silent.

Because every single step up to now had presented a major possible roadblock for us, I hadn't even mentioned the ovulation possibility to Peter. There was no need for him to worry too. Plus, I could sense that he was concerned that I was so optimistic about this attempt at in vitro fertilization. "Ellen, expect the worst but hope for the best" was a phrase he had said twice to me this week on the phone when I excitedly described what I had learned about in vitro each day.

We took the elevator down to the lowest level, then walked close to each other through the tunnel that Sylvia and I had walked two days earlier. I held on to Peter's muscular upper arm. I loved his lean, tanned arms and looped both my arms through his casually, as if we were just walking down the sidewalk from his office toward the Ritz restaurant for dinner after work back home. I was pretending it was only another normal day.

It seemed like just a minute later that we were sitting alone in an examination room. I was wearing a hospital gown, swinging my bare legs, crossed at the ankle. A parade of IVF team members had been in to greet us, as if we were much-anticipated guests at a party.

Dr. Quigley stopped in first on his way to dress for the operating room. He stood very still as if he had all the time in the world to talk with us. He described exactly what the surgical procedure would be for me. First, I would be put under general anesthesia. After I was asleep, an incision would be cut through my navel and the gas would be pumped in to puff up my peritoneum. Dr. Quigley would then insert his tiny laparoscope to locate the ripe eggs on my ovaries. He would aspirate them—gently suck them up—with a pipette. After each was removed, it would be handed over to the embryologist, Dr. Wolf. This was the first time the actual procedure had been explained to me, and I was fascinated. I had tried to find information on the mechanics of the egg-removal procedure before coming to Houston, but this was such a pioneering procedure that none was available.

"Then," Dr. Quigley told Peter, "for the first time, you do not have to sit alone in a waiting room, trying to stop worrying while Ellen has surgery." Peter would be in the room right next to the operating room and would watch some of the procedure on a screen, he added.

"Whoa," Peter balked. I noticed he blanched a few shades lighter right around his lips. "Thanks, but I am not sure I want to see my own wife being operated on." He squished up his mouth as if he had been shown something that repulsed him. Dr. Quigley assured him that would not be the case and that a member of the team would sit with him to explain exactly what he was watching on a screen. Peter would be among a very few people in the entire world to have ever had the opportunity to see an actual human egg.

Before he left, Dr. Quigley made some reference to Georgetown Hoyas sticking together, as they were both graduates from the same university, and I noticed that Peter laughed as he stood to shake the doctor's hand.

Next, Sylvia came in with Rose, who didn't draw blood for once but instead took all of my vitals. I introduced her to Peter as "my new best friend" and showed him my multicolored, bruised arm. He looked horrified, so I made sure he knew that she and I really were able to joke together each day as she drew my blood. I was aware that I had established a unique relationship with the in vitro fertilization team during this intense week. Peter was naturally excluded from this by his absence. So, I brightly introduced him to each member of the medical team the same way I would have at a party where he barely knew anyone.

"Peter, would you pray with me?" We were alone again in the room. I did not know how he would respond.

"Sure, of course," he responded, and I exhaled the breath I had been holding, unsure of his answer.

"Please, God, let this work for us today," I prayed aloud. We each had bowed our heads. I felt an incredible power in my prayer because Peter was joining me in it. "If you let us have a test-tube baby, we promise to tell everyone about this miraculous procedure. Please, God, bless Dr. Quigley and every person on his team today. Please let us have our baby. Amen."

The room just felt different. I was engulfed in complete calm. There was a palpable peace and a powerful, loving confidence that we were not alone in this at all.

Soon I was back on a gurney being wheeled through the familiar swinging doors of a restricted hospital operating area. I had on a green surgical shower cap and was tightly tucked under sheets, like a well-swaddled infant. But today, everything was so different. I was not alone. Peter was walking through the doors right next to me dressed in surgical gear. He had on a green cap, too. This made me ridiculously giddy. He was now totally and completely a part of today's miraculous medical procedure.

My chest, my heart, my complete insides were totally filled by a warm rush of gratitude. It was like swallowing a perfect sip of warm, sweet tea and feeling it slide leisurely down my throat. Dr. Quigley had arranged for Peter to be right there beside me for the very beginnings of our potential child's conception. It was brilliant. It was compassionate and inclusive. If anyone ever dared say to us that creating test-tube babies was taking a couple's love for each other out of the equation and dropping it into a sterile laboratory, we could just laugh, remembering this exact moment.

This extraordinary morning, I was not one bit at risk of being sucked into the undertow of terror that I always had to fight right before surgery. Peter was there, and everyone in the operating room was smiling at both of us. It could not have been more calm or loving. We all were gathered here in this moment for the same reason. We were here to conceive a baby.

The door to an adjoining room was partially open. Inside it I could see a large pull-down screen like the ones I used to show films to my students. Sylvia walked with Peter into the room, talking as they moved, but she did not shut the door. I could see him and hear his voice responding to hers.

I was confident and calm, in a room full of people I knew were on my side. "God is with me, God is guiding me, God is helping me," I repeated slowly inside my head, eyes closed. This reassuring phrase and the familiarity of the message did its job. For the first time ever in an operating room, my body and my mind were joined in serenity. Eyes still closed, I felt the anesthesia smoothly glide through me like honey and I relaxed into the golden haze.

• • •

"Well, hello there, Ellen," I heard a female voice say as my eyes opened. I was already in the recovery room. I blinked and blinked to whisk away the fuzz that covered my eyes like a blanket. I recognized Peter's voice talking somewhere near, just outside of my vision. His voice sounded lighter than his usual serious tone. He laughed. Then, his face appeared at the end of my bed and Dr. Quigley was standing next to him. I blinked a few more times, then tried to force my eyes to stay open. They were both smiling in a conspiratorial way.

Before I could find the words to ask, Dr. Quigley said, "You really did great, Ellen. I was able to aspirate five beautiful eggs."

"And I got to see them," Peter added. "They are gorgeous," he joked. "They look just like you."

"Now what happens?" I asked, trying to make my voice sound strong. It instead sounded like I had just run a race and was winded.

I loved Dr. Quigley's happy brown eyes as he answered. "Dr. Wolf is taking excellent care of your eggs right now in his lab. Sylvia, will you please explain to the Caseys exactly how the procedure continues from here?" I now saw that Sylvia was standing just to the doctor's left, Peter was to his right, and they were smiling as if the three of them were kids who had just had a great adventure they couldn't wait to tell me about. I thought of Huckleberry Finn, Tom Sawyer, and Becky Thatcher.

"Ellen," Dr. Quigley said, "you will just need to finish waking up from the anesthesia. Then you and Peter can go home. Sylvia will stay with you now, and I will get out of my surgical gown and look like a person again instead of the Jolly Green Giant." He looked down at his green scrubs. His mask was still tied on behind his ears and dangling lopsidedly under his chin. I wondered how long it had been since I came out of surgery. It must not have been very long at all. I was awake enough to realize that I was still not awake enough to think clearly. I hated not being completely sharp.

"I will see you day after tomorrow," Dr. Quigley said as he imperceptibly dipped his shoulder to the right in a move to leave. But before he moved, he added kindly, "Can I do anything for you now? Anything?"

"No, thank you," I said. "Thank you so much."

Peter shook hands with the doctor in a congratulatory manner as if they had just watched their team win a ball game together. Dr. Quigley walked off through the quiet recovery room, threading through beds and IV stands. Sylvia pulled the curtains around my bed with a metallic jangle so that she, Peter, and I could speak more privately.

"As Dr. Quigley said, your five eggs are being cared for by Dr. Wolf in the Embryology Lab." I immediately noticed her precise use of the words "your eggs" and "cared for." The eggs were now being treated as alive, belonging to us and treasured by scientists, while no longer inside my body. I had been interested in the psychology driving such precise language, carefully used by this in vitro fertilization team all week. These gentle, new phrases created a shift and certainly evoked the desired result of a protective, nurturing environment.

"Dr. Wolf has each ovum in a separate miniature petri dish," Sylvia continued. "Each dish is carefully labeled with your name, which ovary it was removed from, and which number egg it was in order of aspiration. He will keep them in his incubator in the lab for a few hours and then check to see how they look."

"What do you mean, how they look?" I asked. My mind was clearing rapidly.

"He will examine each embryo under a microscope in four hours from the time of aspiration. After he decides that each individual egg is mature and appears healthy, he will add Peter's sperm to the dish." I immediately wondered how many human eggs Dr. Wolf had ever actually seen. How could he tell if they were healthy and mature? Removing ovum from a woman's ovary was revolutionary. This was the forefront of an innovative medical technology. I was only aware of four programs in the world pioneering IVF. Had he seen other women's eggs right here in Houston? How many other women had tried to have a test-tube baby in Dr. Quigley's experimental program? My mind was racing, full of questions, but I knew I needed to stop wondering and start listening to Sylvia again.

"Then, your eggs will be placed for the night right back into the temperature-controlled incubator that you saw a day ago in Dr. Wolf's lab," she continued. "First thing in the morning, Dr. Wolf will look under the microscope again to see if the eggs are fertilized. I will call you with news as soon as we hear from him. Shall I call your hotel room?"

We nodded. There was no way we would leave that room until we received her call, we both knew, without even needing to ask the other.

• • •

Brrrrring . . . brrrring . . . brrrring.

The shrieking phone pierced my sleep. I jumped forward in a full panic, experiencing the confused horror that only comes from being suddenly awakened in an emergency. Where was I? What was happening?

"I'll get it, unless you want to," Peter said, swinging his legs over the side of the bed and running a hand across his forehead. I was doubled over, holding my shoulder and groaning. The gas from the laparoscopy yesterday was stabbing my left shoulder, in what was now a familiar, jagged pain made worse just now by such a sudden reaction to the phone.

Yesterday's egg retrieval was the fourth laparoscopic procedure I had had in the past four years. The pain was such a stabbing jolt that I felt dewy drops of sweat on my forehead.

"Hi, Sylvia, good morning," Peter was saying as I rocked in agony. I was silent, staring at his back, trying to gauge his reaction to Sylvia's words. He turned sideways and looked at me, nodding. He gave me a thumbs-up signal—and suddenly my pain did not matter. Could it be true?

"All five?" he asked. I didn't move. "Great!"

He listened for what seemed like a long time, then motioned a writing signal with his hand. I jumped out of bed to grab a pen for him to use on the Holiday Inn notepad sitting on his bedside table. He wrote something on the pad, nodding in response to her words. "Okay, then we will keep our fingers crossed and talk with you later this afternoon." He moved his head and eyes up toward my excitedly anxious face. "I think she is fine. Ellen, are you feeling all right?" I nodded.

Peter lay the phone with a clank back onto the cradle. He looked directly at me, exactly the way he did the day we were married. I will always remember the unguarded look of love that day in his green eyes, and I recognized it again in this moment.

"We have five embryos!" The usually reserved Peter stood up in his plaid boxer shorts and pumped his fist. "Woohoo! You did it! We did it! All right!"

I was on the verge of hysterical laughter or hysterical tears but couldn't tell which. The line between the two is so heartbreakingly thin. I pressed the pain in my shoulder down with my right hand and raised my left with a whoop that did not sound like anything I had ever released before in my life. I looked up at the ceiling and whispered, "Thank you, thank you, thank you."

"Tell me everything!" I sat back on the bed and crossed my legs, staring at Peter, who held all of the information I was dying to hear.

"Well, that is pretty much it," Peter responded. Knowing my reticent Peter, he could easily have stopped with that comment. This morning, however, he was too excited to be finished.

"Dr. Wolf just phoned Dr. Quigley's office and said that all five eggs were fertilized when he checked them this morning. The guy must have slept at the lab to examine them so early. Sylvia must have gotten to the office at dawn herself to wait for his call. She said that Dr. Quigley is really pleased. How about that? We really did it."

"Now what happens?"

"So, okay. They rest in the incubator all day today and then Dr. Wolf will check them again this evening. Sylvia will call us with an update tonight. This is amazing, right?" He looked at me, shaking his head in disbelief. "She sounded really happy."

Later that warm summer evening, we drove to a Mexican

restaurant after getting the next thrilling phone call from Sylvia. Our embryos were dividing perfectly. Peter and I were both well educated in the biology of cell division. Mitosis, the process of cell division, occurs as the fertilized egg divides into two cells, then into four cells, and continues dividing. Incredulously, these dividing cells were ours. And this changed everything.

I loved them. I couldn't help it, nor did I try.

I was surprised at the depth of attachment I felt to these teeny embryos that were part Peter, part me. It was a miraculous gift to love each one at a stage when no other human mother could ever have known a child had been conceived.

Inside the female human body, fertilization occurs in the Fallopian tubes. The embryo is then pushed by microscopic hairs through the tube and down to the uterus. In natural conception, silent and unrecognized potential babies would still be floating toward a mother's uterus. Tonight, thanks to this miracle of in vitro fertilization, our embryos were floating in a medium created in a lab from my blood, in tiny plastic dishes inside an incubator. All five of them.

• • •

"Look," Peter said, pointing out the window as the cab cruised along in the dark that evening toward the restaurant where we had dinner reservations. Lights from inside Hermann Hospital and the adjoining buildings created a glow, like a halo, in the darkness. Our babies were in there.

I looked toward the windows, smiling, and secretly winked at them.

Chapter 21

The next morning, I lay very still in a quiet, gently darkened surgery room. It was now two days after my five eggs had been harvested from my ovaries and fertilized. Sylvia had handed me a Valium tablet in a pleated paper cup to swallow with water, sometime within the last hour. I wasn't sure now exactly how long ago, as the effects of the sedative were filling me with a soft drowsiness and feeling of well-being.

Sylvia had sat sideways on a chair in the empty waiting room, and watched as I popped the pill into my mouth and gulped down the glass of water she placed on a table next to me. She explained, in her quiet, Southern manner, how the embryos would soon be transferred into my body by Dr. Quigley. He would thread a tiny pipette through my cervix and push the embryos up in my uterus.

I pictured the plastic toy syringe I had in my little doctor kit as a child. I would fill it with water by pulling out the plunger then squirt all of the water back out through the end.

The Valium would make my mind and body calm and relaxed, Sylvia continued. The in vitro doctors had a new theory that quieting the body with a sedative would help the uterus not reject the embryos. Following the very simple embryo transfer in a few minutes, I would stay in the hospital all this day and through the night, resting.

"Then what?" I asked. "I will be terrified to stand up in the morning for fear the embryos will fall back out."

"They won't fall out," Sylvia smiled patiently.

"Don't you think I should stay lying down for more than twenty-four hours? It just seems like such a risk. I will be afraid to go to the bathroom. I think I should stay in bed for a few more days, just to be sure."

"Well, Ellen, the girls who are pregnant right now only stayed in bed for twenty-four hours." I noticed the slightest spark in Sylvia's eyes as she spoke.

Oh, my God. This program has achieved a pregnancy, I thought. *At least two pregnancies, as she said "girls." Oh, my God. It is true.* My hands began to tingle and I couldn't manage to find any words to respond.

I knew that this extraordinary information had been carefully saved, only to be imparted today. All week I had been noticing and analyzing how small bits of information were parceled out to me. It seemed to be another component of Dr. Quigley's plan to care for the psychological state of the mother going through in vitro.

The mother. There were mothers. This was staggering, game-changing news. Learning it now, on the very morning I was going to have our five live embryos transferred back into my body, filled me with overjoyed confidence. My body could have floated away like a helium balloon, I was so euphoric. No wonder they gave me Valium, I joked to myself.

An intense, physical need to have my embryos back inside of me, where they belonged, and where I could protect them, surged through me smoothly as I began to relax into the tranquilizer. I lay under a warmed blanket on the narrow operating room table, my mind wafting softly like a feather through a light blue haze in the dimly lit room, remembering. I remembered all of it. The four years of heartbreaking loss and brutal pain that had brought me to this room had certainly taken its toll. Every gasping sob, every tear, every scar, every hour spent pouring through medical journals in the library, every second spent in emergency rooms and recovery rooms, every recurring thought of guilt, every single second of anguish would be worth it if today's final, sweet moment of in vitro fertilization led to our success.

Dr. Quigley was sitting on a rolling stool at the end of the bed. A nurse had helped me place my feet in the metal stirrups and a sheet was draped over my knees so that I couldn't actually see him.

A side door opened on my right, causing a beam of pure light to seep into the dimness. I saw a white shoe first, as into the room stepped Sylvia, clad in full medical scrubs and mask. Across her inner forearms, palms facing upward, she was carrying a clean white towel, on which rested a small, clear glass tube. She walked slowly, placing each foot down with great care, as if she were presenting a fragile treasure to the emperor in a fairy tale. She never took her eyes off of the glass. I knew immediately that our embryos were inside that tube. Sylvia was treating the tube like she was honored to have it in her care. She held it in the reverential, loving way I have seen nurses in movies hold precious, naked newborns when handing them into their mothers' arms.

Two weeks later we all knew that what Sylvia cradled so devoutly that morning was indeed a priceless gift, a treasure. She carried a medical miracle inside of a test tube.

She held my baby girl.

A Year and a Half Later

"Wouldn't you say you are playing God?"

Moments earlier, cool fingers had touched my neck as an assistant, wearing big earphones loosely hanging under her chin, clipped a microphone onto my white, ruffled collar. The people I noticed when I arrived this morning, standing in line outside the studio doors in a long hallway, were now settling into their seats. I squinted out, trying to see them, but there were so many lights shining into my eyes and multiple cameramen stepping over cords and blocking my view that I was unable to clearly focus on the guests. The television studio audience was much smaller than I expected, and it looked like they were mostly women, judging by the silk scarves dangling out of the sleeves of their spring coats now draped over the backs of chairs.

Mother always said that red gave a woman confidence, so I had borrowed her red boiled-wool jacket. I had never been on a television program and had spent the evening before in my hotel room studying all of my information on in vitro fertilization. I had carefully kept files with every medical form, newspaper article, letters from doctors' offices, and every one of my own notes starting just after the very first infertility doctor's appointment in 1979.

"Wouldn't you say you are playing God?" She turned with a conspiratorial nod toward the audience as if to have the crowd join her in this aggressive question.

I was well aware of the Irish Catholic makeup of this studio audience in Boston. I knew exactly what I could do to help them understand.

"Oh, no, I thank God for the gifted doctors and medical researchers who made it possible for my husband and me to finally have our own baby."

"How can you possibly say that producing a child in a test tube isn't playing God?" she continued.

"This is no different than a heart bypass," I replied. "This is simply a bypass of the Fallopian tubes. My egg couldn't reach the uterus, just as blood can't flow through a blocked heart artery. We are so grateful to God for the scientific discovery of this miraculous procedure. I am on your program today so other couples know they have a chance to have their own baby, thanks to the God-given gift of in vitro fertilization."

Dr. Quigley shared, with my permission, our home phone number with the attorney and author Lori Andrews. She had interviewed me by phone when I was five months pregnant. One chapter of her book *New Conceptions* was about Peter's and my quest to have our own child. Lori was on the panel with me today, and I could see her sitting motionless, wondering and worrying how I would handle this barrage of questions. It was like I was being cross-examined in a witness-box.

"Playing God," the TV host repeated.

I felt my head shake in an involuntary "no" movement, not in answer to her shock-value question, but as a sign of disappointment.

There were so many deeply private questions I wish the host had asked—questions only I and the handful of other mothers of in vitro babies could have answered. Had I been concerned over publicity when "Colorado's first test-tube baby" appeared in headlines around the country? I would have described how, at 1 AM, just twenty-four hours after my baby's birth, I pressed my emergency call button in the darkened maternity ward. I had been awakened by the shock of desperately needing to protect my defenseless newborn child as she slept, away from me, in the nursery. I squeezed the nurse's hand in my shaking one and held her eyes as I begged her to keep special guard over my precious infant. I had been crushed under an avalanche of terror that my baby would be kidnapped once news of her birth was released.

I would have frowned reflectively and looked down at my lap as I confessed that I searched the Letters to the Editor section in secret daily for months after our baby was born. I loudly flapped the newspaper pages open each morning with both hands, my heart banging in dread that there would be a letter saying that test-tube babies were a blasphemy. I was prepared to defend all of us, our new family, my doctors, and the silent parents of IVF babies who never had told anyone how their child was conceived.

I refused to grant the press permission to use our last name, and I wasn't ashamed of that. While I didn't believe in anonymity for my sake, I was, perhaps irrationally, perhaps not, petrified for my baby's safety. An imagined person or group might strike us with words or worse because of how our child had been conceived. That fear froze so deeply in my body that there were moments when my bones felt as if they were coated in ice. Yet I never once whispered this private terror to a soul—not to Peter, my mother, or my friends. I shuddered in that cold alone.

Onstage that day, I was prepared to share with other families what it had been like for me, one of the first mothers in the world to give birth to a baby conceived in vitro, had the interviewer asked those relevant questions. Instead, she was disappointing me.

She might have asked if I had a normal pregnancy and birth. I would have described the easiest pregnancy ever and a labor of only three total hours. It would have been of medical interest to describe how I got to have more ultrasounds than other pregnant women, and how the doctor carefully measured the size of my fetus's skull and sent the information to Dr. Quigley in Houston. I suspected there was a concern about the as-yet-unknown health and development of in vitro babies, which was being intensely studied. I never once had a moment of worry about my baby's health. Peter called me "The Walking Smile" for nine months.

"You had five embryos," she could have said. "What happened to the other four?" Only one of the five embryos transferred had implanted in my uterus wall. Doctors believed that fertilized eggs often do not implant in a woman's cycle, for reasons still being studied.

I would have loved to answer another question she didn't ask, "What misconceptions about in vitro have you faced?" I could have chuckled as I related my answers to "Where is the baby growing?" (when I was clearly eight months pregnant), "Who is the father?" and "Is the baby in a jar in a lab right now in Houston?"

If only the talk show host had just thoughtfully asked, "But you were the first in Colorado, a pioneer; didn't you feel completely alone?"

I would have said yes. My heart would forever remember that I had been alone in my grief, my guilt, and my single-minded determination. Though I had the support of my husband, family, and friends, it was just me being wheeled into the operating room every single time. I was alone when I had microsurgery, a medical technique no one I knew had ever heard of. Alone in Hartford Hospital, I was one of the very first women to have laser surgery on Fallopian tubes. I went into the in vitro fertilization program in Houston completely alone, knowing of only four other women in the world who had been through the same procedure. There were certainly other women going through each of these experimental surgeries, but I never, ever met one in the hospital or in the waiting room of a doctor's office.

I had been totally on my own, but now, others didn't have to be. For all of the women coming behind me, sitting in that audience, or watching from home—the unseen, bereft women I would never know personally, who desperately wanted a baby, who needed information on what nascent techniques were available and where they were being performed, women not sure where to go, whom to ask—I was here to tell them.

I had quite a story to tell.

Acknowledgments

Always at the top of my list, I thank my spectacular, talented, accomplished daughter, Elizabeth Casey, who is the finest person I know. Integrity, intelligence, and determination have been a thread in your life since the day you were born. It is the honor and privilege of my life to be your mother. Thank you for your journalistic assistance as I wrote this book and your sense of humor when I was frustrated.

Peter Casey, you stuck by me every day through this difficult, incredible journey. You never said "no," but selflessly helped me follow my dream of having our own baby. When Elizabeth gave birth to our grandson, Bennett, you said, "Ellen, this is all thanks to you," and my heart broke just a bit, remembering all the times you sat alone in a hospital waiting room. Thank you.

Dr. John M. Smith, if not for you I would not have had my baby. You consistently treated me with respect for my intelligence and dignity as a female patient. You took extra care to save my ovaries in the multiple emergency surgeries you performed on me, preserving my ability to have a child. Your book, *Women and Doctors* (The Atlantic Monthly Press, 1992), is a gift to all women. It exposes the abuse of women by male ob-gyn physicians. Your book warns female readers against exactly the type of unethical marketing that misled me as a young, unmarried twenty-four-year-old woman to use the test IUD. Dr. Smith, you are a hero in my life. Thank you.

Thank you to my daughter, Elizabeth, and her husband, Ryan Ward, who acted as my personal tech support team every time I had problems with my computer or printer. Thank you to my dear friends who were readers and supporters: Anne Dessert, Jacque Walsh, Kathy Gilbert, Carol Meyer, Chris Hannan. Thank you, Jacquie Cobb, who introduced me as "the mother of Colorado's first test-tube baby" at her backyard party. The ensuing conversation inspired me to write this memoir.

Elizabeth Brown, you are a superb editor and understood my book from the moment you began editing. To the professional, creative, supportive team at Greenleaf Books/River Grove: Tyler LeBleu, Lindsey Clark, Chelsea Richards, David Endris, Sam Ofman, Neil Gonzales, and Tiffany Barrientos, who made this book a reality. Thank you for bringing my story into the hands of readers everywhere.

An enormous thank-you goes to Adrienne Brodeur and the staff at the Aspen Institute Summer Words program, who encouraged and supported this book every step of the way. Your intensive program for writers is beyond compare. Thank you to the writing coach and author Karen Bender, who helped get my project started smoothly. Thank you, Grace Freedson, for your help navigating the literary publishing world.

Thank you to Dr. Robin Johnson, Dr. Creed Wyatt, and Thomas "Rusty" Pool, PhD, the medical professionals who helped me discover the latest in IVF lab technology, radiology diagnosis in ectopic pregnancy, and ectopic intervention treatments. Hugs to Sue Downey, who provided details of the Connecticut landscape. A special thank-you goes to two devoted friends, Sally Howard and Claire Hicks, who were by my side from the very beginning of my odyssey to become a mother.

I credit much of my success in life to my alma mater, Laurel School for Girls, in Shaker Heights, Ohio, where it was ingrained in me to always believe in myself and make my own decisions. It was because of this progressive education that I knew to question male medical authority, research solutions for difficult problems, and fulfill my obligation to make a difference in the world.

Mother, your love for me and for your granddaughter, Elizabeth, will always be a constant in our lives. We adore you forever.

About the Author

 **Ellen Weir Casey** is an award-winning educator and writer who has dedicated her life to teaching, nurturing, and inspiring children. She made headlines as the "mother of Colorado's miracle baby" in 1983. She has spoken about her experience as an in vitro pioneer on national television and in national print media.

She is a graduate of Colorado College, earning both a BA in English and a master's degree in education. Ellen is delighted when she is still introduced today as the mother of "Colorado's first test-tube baby." She lives in the shadow of Pikes Peak, in the foothills of Colorado Springs. Her newest role as grandmother to Bennett is the icing on the cake of her life.